SEXUAL HAPPINESS

By

Donald L. Boone

INTRODUCTION

This book is to help those who are seeking the correct sexual mate in their lives, a person who can bring them sexual fulfilment. This is an age-old dilemma that has plagued men, and women alike since the beginning of time. Most of the time the problem of finding the best person for your life can be overcome with a careful selection, and this book is designed to help you bring that about. This book is assembled slightly differently from most other books of this kind in that I've started with the first month of the year, rather than with the third, which is customary

There are a few things you need to be aware of before you begin your search for the person you want in your life for the years ahead. The most important thing you personally need during your search for someone is self confidence. Why self confidence you may ask, here is the reason why. We, as human beings are afraid of rejection. We are afraid of being told we are not desirable and it doesn't matter whom it is that telling us. To find the right mate you need self confidence because you have to ask very personal questions and you want really honest and satisfying answers to help you make your choices.

What most often happens is that while we speak to others in a personal manner, we ask questions in such a way as to avoid, being given negative answers. No matter what it relates to. However, when you are making a choice involving your happiness, and your future, you must get over the fear of rejection. It is far better to be disappointed, occasionally during your search, than to be bitterly unhappy with having made an unwise choice. You have to overcome the fear of being told, in any manner and one way or another. "You're not desirable, to me." For those that choose incorrectly and still make a commitment, one may be happy, or contented, while the other person begins to feel the unrest of the relationship. Over time this will end up as a separation with both people looking anew.

In your choosing of a mate, try not to look at the physical attractiveness of the person as the physical appearance will not matter over time. Look instead at their behavior, how he, or she, treats others. Is there a temper problem, if there is, do not think you can cure it, or put up with it? You cannot. Or are there problems with mind-altering drugs of any kind, or the taking of unnecessary chances. Any negative behavior should be viewed seriously. It is a proven fact that more relationships are first based physical appearance, and on one's sense of humor more than anything else. But, is that enough? No, it isn't.

Once you find someone whom you are interested in, and have spent enough time in their company to have made the decision to get personal, get over any fear of rejection. You need to ask the questions that pertain to your desires, or make the statements that will move your relationship forward. The conversation you undertake with this person will be of a very personal nature, and it can often be quite blunt in the terms of language.

Blunt to the point that the questions you ask should bring truthful blunt answers. Now is the time to find out if they like oral sex, perhaps kinky sex, or what do they enjoy sexually. If it doesn't fit your own needs, then you can move along on your path in search of the one who does fit your needs. The conversations may be lengthy, or short, depending on how the relationship proceeds. But, the more direct you are in the beginning, the sooner you will have the answers you need. Don't avoid this part of the discovery no matter how bashful you may be, or inhibited. This is crucial information to your well being. Believe me.

The list I provide for you here will be in sequence on a monthly basis, rather than in astrological order. Each person listed will have an explanation as to their own general needs. The old saying. "What's your Sign?" Carries more information than you might have imagined possible. The first section of the book deals with the individual nature of people, the second section will explain how you find out their personality, and this is quite often very important information.

Table of contents

Introduction

Aries   March - April 30
          Men
          Women
          Marriage
          Natural tendencies
          Suggestions to Consider
          Special notes
          Fundamentals
          Physical
          Emotion
          Mental

Taurus   April - May   .38
          Men
          Women
          Marriage
          Natural tendencies
          Suggestions to Consider
          Special notes
          Fundamentals
          Physical
          Emotion
          Mental

Leo   July - August .71
          Men
          Women
          Marriage
          Natural tendencies
          Suggestions to Consider
          Special notes
          Fundamentals
          Physical
          Emotion
          Mental

Virgo   August - September .80
          Men
          Women
          Marriage
          Natural tendencies
          Suggestions to Consider
          Special notes
          Fundamentals
          Physical
          Emotion
          Mental

SECTION ONE
INDIVIDUALS

This first section explains how each individual feels, or reacts to their own sexual world. However, you must remember that this is not what their personality might exhibit, as that side of their nature will alter their likes and dislikes to some degree. This first section will tell you a great deal of useful information, perhaps all you feel you need, but look through section two as well. Section two will explain how to figure out someone's personality as well. Once you have that knowledge you can use the information in the book to give you a much clearer understanding of the person you are dealing with. Section one will be useful in finding the person you want in the beginning, section two will help you fully understand the person you have found.

✭
JANUARY - FEBRUARY
MEN
AQUARIUS

The Aquarian male is a man you will rarely find to be a dull person and you will never know what is about to take place next in life while you are with this man. This is someone who thinks well into the future, and way ahead of most others. This is possibly one of the most attractive looking men of the zodiac. This man may take you to a fast food place for lunch and then a very nice place for dinner. You may be in for a movie for the evenings entertainment, or perhaps live theaters, even a museum. Perhaps you might find yourself at a planetarium for something far different from the normal kind of entertainment. This unusual individual can cry during a thirty-second television commercial, and seem cold and distant toward others the next.

Though it may be rare, this can be a shy individual, and he can easily enjoy solitude.   He is very independent, self sufficient, and he rebels against the norm as a matter of a normal course. Therefore, when it comes to this person as a lover you can feel free to experiment and to use your imagination. To do so could produce some very enjoyable, and memorable love experiences. Perhaps for both of you. Be aware of yourself with this man as he will show you things about yourself you were never aware of before. If you'll let him and b e open minded, he may surprise you sexually. As this man will find pleasure in giving you pleasure. You will gain more self-gratification by learning to pleasure him as well, and don't be bashful. He will enjoy it if you make the play first. Aquarians are not known for being highly sexual, however, if Venus is in Aquarius, or Capricorn at the time of his birth you could find yourself with a sexual animal. When you sleep with this man, you can expect his leg to be across yours during the night, or his hand cupping your breast.

WOMEN
AQUARIUS
This woman is not impressed by the strong
athletic broad-shouldered type of man, as she
prefers men who exhibit an interesting character,
and perhaps those who seem somewhat cultured.
She does not care if a man really has apparent
sex appeal as she most often sees the true man
for whom, and what he is. She herself is someone
can awaken the appetite of men who know about
women. This is one of the most liberated women
on sexual issues that you may ever meet.

She can join any conversation and can soon be in
control of the discussion, or the topic of the
discussion. She may occasionally seem, and may
be, egotistical and arrogant. Yet she has the
smarts to back it up. It doesn't matter if she is the
center of attraction, or even if she has been
placed there by others. You'll see by her very
nature she is often brought into the limelight. You
may never know who this woman is from week to
week. She might be one of the sixty's hippie's
type one day, and a well-spoken high class
woman of quality the next. Does this woman have
morals, absolutely, well at least until they get in
her way. If her marriage or relationship is
suffering, she may find herself interested in other
men, men who are intellectually attractive. You
must understand, this woman is a very dedicated
partner, but, she doesn't confuse love and sex,
because she is well aware they are two different
things. Aquarians are not known for being highly

sexual, however, if Venus is in Aquarius, or Capricorn at the time of their birth you could find yourself with a sexual animal on your hands. When you sleep with this woman, you may find her hand holding onto you, waiting for any stirring that might take place. If you want to entertain this woman, you better expect to be doing something different, something unusual, and something outside of the realm of what is considered to be the norm. As an example, where you might take one woman to a movie, you take the Aquarian woman to a show at the planetarium. Where you go for a drive with other women, you take this woman sailing. I think you get the picture.

MARRIAGE

This can be a choosy marital partner. If this is
your mate it may have taken him or her, some
time to find you because they often search for
their mates. The wise ones do not rush into
marriage. They don't rush because they are too
choosy. Once married to the correct mate, it will
be a rare Aquarian to wander from the marital
bed. This may be because they are often very
busy taking care of the world. There can be
problems having this person as your mate, some
of those are as follows.

This Sun sign doesn't like to work hard. It is for
this reason that is why there are more inventors
from this group than any of the other sun signs.
They invent things so they won't have to work so
hard. It goes without question that this is a
humanitarian. This person will be so busy doing
good, that his or her own family may lack some of
this caring attitude at home. Can they make
mistakes, of course not, just ask one of them.
Well, none that they will admit to, especially if they
have some planets in Virgo. One other factor with
this sun sign, they are often found in interracial
relationships.

The male of this Sun sign, may have a wandering
eye for the opposite sex. Though he may not have
the tendency to having an indiscreet affair, he will.
He would rather, if possible, make it a legal
joining.

NATURAL TENDENCIES
Some think that Aquarians are not an overly
sexual sun sign, however Aquarians who have
Venus in the signs of Aquarius or Capricorn, are
well aware of their sexual needs. If the planet
Venus should fall into their first house, their
sexual drive can be closer to addiction. This is a
condition they live with their entire lives, and it is
on their mind constantly. When age, or any other
factor strikes down their sexual ability it drives
them crazy. They know they can no longer
perform in the bedroom as they did in the past,
but in their minds all is still well, and the sex drive
continues.

This is a person who likes being seen naked. If
you are this person, you may want to consider the
sun signs born between October and March.
These sun signs may have similar sexual needs
such as yourself. During these months Venus can
be found in Aries, which will be aggressive in the
search for sexual mate who can keep up with
them. Venus in Scorpio can produce a high
sexual appetite, almost to the point of
Nymphomania.

Venus in Capricorn is a social sexual need that is
this may be someone who wants to make love to
everyone in their social circle. An Aquarius is also
someone who wants to love everyone and may try
to do so. This could be the sun sign that started
the idea of having a harem to feed the sexual
appetite. Through the years as a youth this sun

sign learns how to treat the opposite sex, the charming attitude, the charisma all become ways to entice the opposite sex into bed. Even while involved in a relationship, of any kind, this is someone who can find themselves in bed with someone else.

SUGGESTIONS TO CONSIDER

It has been said that the air signs, Gemini, Libra and Aquarius can get along with anyone, and basically this is true. However, when they choose a mate who is also an air sign they are seldom true to each other, mainly because the relationship is, in a sense, tame. Still, if the two people have the planet Venus in the same sign at the time of birth, their sexual outlook is often the same. This can bring sexual harmony and with this can come sexual contentment. Aquarians can get along well with an Aries, but the Aries will have to be the one to start the sexual fires of Aquarius burning. The same would be true for a Leo sun sign involved with an Aquarian. A Sagittarius is another good sign for Aquarius to get involved with.

If you are born as this sun sign, and a highly sexual person you may want to consider those born between October and March as this is the time of the year when Venus is in the sun signs noted for addiction of any kind. Sexual addiction is not unlike any other kind of mind-altering drug. If you find someone to your liking don't make a long term commitment until you are certain the relationship will work out to your satisfaction. You should also be sure you are capable of fulfilling their needs as well. You do not have to heed the recommended sun signs for each group you find listed here in this book, but history tells us it is best.

SPECIAL NOTES

This is usually the most attractive sign of the Zodiac, but this natural attractiveness comes with its own problems. Because of the beauty of this sign, both men and women are, in a sense afraid of them. Not as human beings, but because they think of this sign as beyond them. We as humans are afraid of rejection. To ask this person out on a date or for private time together, many often make the opposite sex feel inadequate. It's as if this person is beyond our reach. Nothing can be farther from the truth. Physical beauty comes with a price tag as well, that of being left alone. Because of the fear of rejection on other peoples part, this can be a lonely person and they crave relationships. In reality this is probably one of the easiest sun signs to approach for getting together.

Aquarians are known to be altruistic, and a humanitarian by nature. In general they love mankind. This actually goes a little further than a generalization, as it is most Aquarians do not love one tree in the forest, they love the whole forest. It is the same condition with the opposite sex. Their open mindedness allows them to experience many avenues of sexual exploration. This may come about by the urging of a sexual partner who wants to teach them new ways to enjoy themselves. What others think of as, 'Kinky sex,' can be accepted by an Aquarian as perfectly normal. This is a person who likes being seen naked. To the point that they may flash their private parts, or just accidentally allow themselves to be seen in some manner. It turns them on sexually.

Aquarians are no different from many other signs of the zodiac in that they can be quite noisy while they are making love, especially when they reach their peak and climax. To make love outside is a stimulating experience for them as well and they may find they experience more intense climaxes out in the open. It's as if they are exhibiting themselves for any or all to see. This is one of the sun signs that can fall into a group who becomes addicted to sex. If this is the case, it will be a common thing for them to masturbate. Perhaps every day. As someone who enjoys sex a great deal, oral sex is a natural method of sexual pleasure. Receiving from, or giving to a partner. Pornography, or pornographic stories, will be a big sexual turn on for them but it brings the need for gratification soon after. To say they are promiscuous may be erroneous, but it can happen. If, at the time of birth, Venus was in the signs of Capricorn or Aquarius, they may have an ongoing need for sexual gratification.

If you are the lover of a Dual sign, or its opposite sign, such as a Gemini / Sagittarius, or Virgo / Pisces, don't expect to be their only lover. Dual signs also mean, dual relationships. This is someone who can become involved in incestuous relationships, even if it is not they, who start them along this path.

FUNDAMENTALS
AQUARIUS

This sun sign has a marked influence with the eleventh house in a horoscope. This is the house of friends. This person is the do gooder, the good guy, and the humanitarian. An odd thing about this sun sign is the fact that in almost every interracial relationship one of the two people will be of this sun sign, or have it on the ascendant, which is the personality. A cancer sun sign is another one found in interracial relationships. Aquarians are ruled by the planet Uranus, which produces constant changes of some kind.

This will be something different from what most others would consider as different. If, you know one of these people you will often find you have never met someone like them before, nor will there be another one quite like the one you know now. One final note here, they do not love one tree, they love the whole forest. It takes a good mate to help them take root.

PHYSICAL CHARACTERISTICS
AQUARIUS
They have a broad forehead, but not overly large; the eyes are expressive and widely set. They have a good complexion though their teeth are often defective. Their hair grays early and they have a mouth and chin which are attractive. This is a person who has considerable physical beauty, and they are vivacious.

EMOTIONAL CHARACTERISTICS
AQUARIUS
The emotional and compassionate nature is very strong, but in the negative types of Aquarians it is not very profound. These are lively, excitable people with a kindly disposition. They are well-liked, gentle, and altruistic. They are basically domestic but changeable. They are also an unconventional, temperamental, worrying group.

MENTAL CHARACTERISTICS
AQUARIUS
Inventive, intellectual, and fond of literature and science. They are diplomatic, tolerant, reasonable, independent, and discreet. Continued optimism, a humanitarian, but fixed opinions, foreseeing way ahead of others, but they can become confused in an emergency perhaps can be superficial at times.

✮

FEBRUARY - MARCH
MEN
PISCES

There may be some unusual times spent with this individual, and make no mistake he can be moody. Look closely and you might be able to see his moods change in the depth of his eyes. There will be times in life when he will seem to know what is about to happen before it takes place. This man can easily go unnoticed by others often due to his ability to create a feeling in others that he does not exist in their presence, as if invisible. He will enjoy the water, and living around, or even on it, as it has a soothing effect on him. Going fishing will erase all and drain all tension or worries from his mind. He can be a very social, or a very secluded kind of person. This is often the one man to whom other people talk too about their own problems. His physical involvement's are in tune with his emotional involvement's. He may be drawn into any kind of love situation just to get closer to his mate. This man needs to be constantly aware of his mate, and of her intentions especially toward him, as he can lose himself in the relationship.

WOMEN
PISCES
It is not uncommon for this woman to be sexually demanding and unpredictable in her sexual needs. Those needs may differ from day to day, and the various moods may come and go. Sometimes she may have great sexual desires for months, then she may do without for a length of time. This condition can drive her, and her mate, to an uneasy relationship. She can just as easily live in a world of fantasy, and may not dare, or have a fear of leaving it for the reality of life.

The man who has an imagination, and is exploratory, has a good chance in winning this woman. The right man can find himself with a sex slave, or, does he become the sex slave during their lovemaking? At times she can be slow to try new things, but once she finds the pleasure in them they will become more to her liking. This can really be the whore in the bedroom, and the quiet maiden in the living room. You will find she likes a man's hands exploring her breasts and she may make them readily available for this purpose. This is also a person who likes being seen naked. To the point that they may flash their private parts, or just accidentally allow themselves to be seen in some manner as it turns them on sexually. If you become her first mate, you should know she can discover you are not who she thought you were in the beginning. If this happens, you will become a history. If you are her second mate, you stand a better chance of survival as her mate, but you have to accept her the way she is. You should not offer any rejection of her, or you too, may also become history. It's not that she can't take rejection, she can but it must be done in a constructive manner.

MARRIAGE

It may seem that a Pisces will marry any Sun sign and they might, but it is a necessity for this Sun sign to marry correctly to attain marital bliss. They need someone who understands their sensitivities and their day dreaming of better things to come. Even if they don't take place. They build castles in the air as they have a pie in the sky attitude. To those who wed this Sun sign will find that just being a Pisces can be a curse as their emotional state can be a senseless well as full of endless emotions. Still, this Sun sign is probably one of the most charitable sun signs of all.

Some of the problems with having this Sun sign as your mate are as follows.
This is not always the case, but this is a sun sign that can produce a problem drinker, or a user of mind-altering drugs. This can lead to several problems, perhaps often straying from the marital bed, not to mention the addictions they can encounter. If they have Venus in Aquarius, you'll have to take care of their bedroom needs as well.

This is someone similar to that of the Cancer, or Scorpio Sun signs, in the sense that they will seem to be suffering in some manner. They can suffer from anything they want when the excuse is needed. You may never know what it will be that they suffer from, how can you possibly know, they don't know either. Cancer will cry, Scorpios will blame you, but Pisces does not know who's at fault.

NATURAL TENDENCIES

This is someone who reeks of sex appeal and can have an obsessive way of thinking about sex. Often while speaking to a Pisces you become aware of an open suggestion as to having a sexual interlude, but without actually having said the words themselves. It is an illusion they are able to create easily, and no, they don't practice this way of speaking it just comes to them naturally. This leaves it open for a suitor to make an advance without question, or rejection. Pisces are good lovers and they need love in return. This is a person who others take advantage of, it's as if they create a falsehood in their own minds about the one who is using them, as if that person is pure of heart and innocent of harming others. The Pisces can appear as if they are the greatest lovers to come along. The illusion is that they will provide you with a time in bed that you never dreamed of being possible, and they may be successful at doing so. There is often a side to this sign that goes unnotched, but they seem to do better with a lover who provides some domination over them.

SUGGESTIONS TO CONSIDER

The water signs, Cancer, Scorpio and Pisces are a very emotional group pf people. They may also find it difficult to express themselves on a sexual basis unless they have the correct mate. Especially if in a relationship with another water sign. Still, if the two people have the planet Venus in the same sign at the time of birth, their sexual outlook is often the same. This can bring sexual harmony and with this can come sexual contentment. Pisces will find a Taurus much to their liking. As the love making by a Taurus can be very stimulating, it will often be their unusual interests in sex that can excite a Pisces. As Pisces enjoys a hands on approach, they will find a Virgo is a good mate. As Virgo is good with handling and caressing their partners. It is not unusual for a Pisces to find a good relationship with a Capricorn as a lover, and mate.

If you are a highly sexual person you may want to consider those born between October and March as this is the time of the year when Venus is in the sun signs noted for addiction of any kind. Sexual addiction is not unlike any other kind of mind-altering drug. If you find someone to your liking don't make a long term commitment until you are certain the relationship will work out to your satisfaction. You should also be sure you are capable of fulfilling their personal needs as well. You do not have to heed the recommended sun signs for each group you find listed here in this book, but history tells us it is best.

SPECIAL NOTES

A Pisces sun sign is someone who fantasizes about many things in life. Sex is no different. As a dual sun sign a Pisces will find themselves considering more than one sexual partner at a time. Perhaps at the same time, and not necessarily of the same sex. This is a sun sign that is very familiar with promiscuity and it doesn't mean they expect to find themselves in a long term relationship. This is more common than many might think, and to a Pisces it is not something to be ashamed of, sexual enjoyment happens in many ways. They enjoy sexual stimulation through the viewing, or reading of pornographic materials and if they don't have a sexual partner at the moment, they will masturbate to bring about the gratification of a climax. This is why many women of this sun sign have sexual toys, such as a dildo and most likely one that vibrates. Do they enjoy oral sex, without a doubt they do. It seems they really enjoy a sexual partner who talks nasty to them, especially while in the sexual act itself. No matter where it may be, a whispered comment in their ear that alludes to the taking them to bed, is a turn on. If, at the time of birth, Venus was in the sign of Aquarius, this person may have an ongoing need for sexual gratification. Even while involved in a relationship of any kind, this is someone who can find themselves in bed with someone else.

FUNDAMENTALS
PISCES

In astrology, Pisces is ruled by Neptune, the planet of illusion. You may never quite know who this person really is. The problem many Pisceans' have is in reality, even knowing themselves. Self truths are often hidden, or revealed by this planet as it rules the twelfth house of the hidden, or unseen things. The planet Neptune rules Pisces and it creates illusion, or fantasies for the Pisces person to enjoy, or may even need for stimulation. Anything that brings on a mind-altering state of mind. Mind alternating drugs should absolutely be avoided by this person. Escape is not what they need. They need reality.

PHYSICAL CHARACTERISTICS
PISCES

Most often they have a pale complexion and their eyes are often a light blue, or light in color and with great depth. It's as if you can look deep within them merely by looking into their eyes. Their necks are often short with dark hair on their heads and well-shaped lips that set off their face. Their posture may not be good as they may appear to have stooped shoulders and an odd walk.

EMOTIONAL CHARACTERISTICS
PISCES

The emotions may seem to be inhibited, but it can seem this way as this is a sensitive and impressionable person. Pisces often have a psychic ability which can be misunderstood. Most of them will pay attention to their hunches and act on them. This is also a "See poor me suffer." sun sign, often suffering from melancholy.

MENTAL CHARACTERISTICS
PISCES

Theoretical, intuitive, compassionate, introspective, and quick in understanding things. They are philosophic, often religious or involved in some kind of cult. Clairvoyance is indeed possible. They are versatile, talkative, often impractical, good at procrastinating, and may lack of confidence.

★
MARCH - APRIL
MEN
ARIES
These are aggressive and assertive men. If these individuals choose you, they will pursue you relentlessly. When you are his chosen one, this man is interested in results so you should not expect a great deal of foreplay ahead of time. For this man a sexual encounter is a matter of sudden impulse, he may not actually start seeking out a lover, but when he finds her, he will want her right then. He appreciates a woman who lets him know when she can be had, but he will be the dominating mate. Aries men tend to seek out weaker women, women they can impress with their masculinity and women they can protect. For entertainment, this man will take you to events that may require daring on your part. Such as white water river rafting, Bungee jumping, four wheeling in a jeep with the guys, sky diving, hang gliding and any other similar events. If you are withdrawn, a fraidy cat, or afraid of getting hurt, stay home. Of course, it is possible that this is what has drawn him toward you, or you to him. If you are a single mother with children, you need to ask yourself, are your children dare devils, or do they prefer the quiet of good music, a book, or local theater.

WOMEN
ARIES

These are women who possess strong
personalities, to think of this as a namby pamby
woman is an error. This is not a woman just any
man can get along with. It is because this woman
is not going to try to be your equal, she is your
equal. A few who know her will call her. "Bossy."
She is smart, and can work you into the ground,
and then she will wonder why you cannot keep up
with her. After all, she is only a woman.

You will probably be drawn to her personal
magnetism and charisma, but you must
remember she will not be stopping to take care of
you. She has things to get done in her life and will
seldom waist time on trivial things, even weak
men. If this woman wants you, odds are she'll
have you. Then, if you don't measure up, she'll
discard you just as quickly. If she starts an
argument with you, it will be to see if you are
strong enough to stand up to her, if you cave in
mercilessly, you lose. This woman may ask you
point blank if you want to go to bed with her, and
odds are this is not a test. Either you do, or you
don't. It may surprise men that she can be blunt in
her approach, but that is the way she behaves
when she feels the need. She may invite a man of
interest to her to experience something of a
daring escapade. If he hesitates, she will know he
may be too weak for her and she's not going to
waste any more time on her pursuit of this male.

MARRIAGE

Some of the problems with having this Sun sign as your mate, are as follows.

This is someone who can fall in love quickly, and they fall out just as quickly. They may show a jealous streak you didn't know was there before you married them, but you will find out if the Aries thinks you are getting too chummy with anyone else. Had they been married before you came along, odds are they were. Odds are they will be married again after you have left their marital bed.

This, is someone who lives for a danger of some sort. Though they may not think of their chosen path as all that dangerous. Though you, or I, wouldn't try doing the same thing. This is an easier sign for men than for women. The men need a weaker mate who is satisfied to remain in the background. An Aries woman is often too strong for most men, yet she needs a strong mate. Not a mate to rule her, well not all of the time anyway, but a mate who can stand up to her, and hold his own.

NATURAL TENDENCIES

Aries who have Venus in the signs of Aries or
even Taurus can have strong sexual desires. If
this planet should fall into their first house, which
is the house of our physical body, their sexual
drive can be one to produce a constant need. This
is one of the sun signs that can also fall into a
group who can become addicted to sex. This is a
condition they live with their entire lives, but it
carries a few problems with it as well. An aries
has the tendency to jump into relationships before
then should. If they do not have a lover who can
meet their needs, they will abandon the
relationship just as quickly as they entered into it,
no matter how the other person feels. This person
may want to consider the sun signs born between
October and March. These sun signs may have
similar sexual needs. During these months Venus
can be found in Aries, which will be aggressive in
the search for sexual mate who can keep up with
them. Venus in Scorpio can produce a high
sexual appetite, almost to the point of
Nymphomania. Venus in Capricorn is a social
sexual need that is this may be someone who
wants to make love to everyone in their social
circle. An Aquarius is also someone who wants to
love everyone, and may try to do so.

SUGGESTIONS TO CONSIDER
The fire signs, Aries, Leo and Sagittarius are exceedingly passionate, but when they mate with other fire signs there is a constant ongoing battle for supremacy between the two of them. The clash that takes place between them will usually drive them apart. Still, if the two people have the planet Venus in the same sign at the time of birth, their sexual outlook is often the same. This can bring sexual harmony, and with this can come sexual contentment once they understand who the boss is in the relationship. Aries gets along well with the air signs. It may be because the air signs often need the push that an aggressive Aries is known for.

If you are a highly sexual person you may want to consider those born between October and March as this is the time of the year when Venus is in the sun signs noted for addiction of any kind. Sexual addiction is not unlike any other kind of mind-altering drug. If you find someone to your liking don't make a long term commitment until you are certain the relationship will work out to your satisfaction. You should also be sure you are capable of fulfilling their needs as well. You do not have to heed the recommended sun signs for each group you find listed here in this book, but history tells us it is best.

SPECIAL NOTES

The aries sun sign is one of a natural assertiveness. When they decide on someone they want as a lover, it may be hard for them to give up the chase even when it becomes necessary. There's an old saying you might want to heed. It goes like this. "Don't pursue someone who does not want to be caught." Even while involved in a relationship, of any kind, this is someone who can suddenly find themselves in bed with someone else.

No matter which sex you are, male of female, An Aries enjoys being the person on top in the missionary position. They can also be a very verbal, or a noisy lover when they reach their peak and climax. Though many sun signs will make love any time of day, an Aries prefers to make love in the mornings. And, when they masturbate, it will most often be in bed in the mornings as well. The women of this sun sign often enjoy sexual toys, with perhaps some interest in methods of restraining lovers, such as with handcuffs or a soft rope.

If you are the lover of a Dual sign, or its opposite sign, such as Gemini / Sagittarius, or Virgo / Pisces, don't expect to be their only lover. Dual signs also means, dual relationships.

FUNDAMENTALS
ARIES

This is someone who charges headlong into those who oppose them and is not concerned about winning or losing, well perhaps there may be some concern about losing. Mainly because that rarely happens. This is an aggressive person, arrogant, pushy, daring and unafraid. Aries controls the first house in the basic natal chart, that of the physical body, and this can be a daring person. So when this person has any planets in this sign, those planets too will display the same assertive tendencies. Someone with Venus in Aries is a person who is not willing to take "No." For an answer. Man, or woman. If this is someone who desires another person physically, odds are they will succeed in having that person. Mercury in Aries would produce a person who does not think in terms of doing things the easy way, just to accomplish the task. In the world of business this is the person who gets things done, and gains the respect of those above, and below him, or her. Never mind the chaos that may have just barely been avoided through a chancy move.

PHYSICAL CHARACTERISTICS
ARIES

They have long necks and an angular face with high cheek bones and with a narrow chin. Their eyes are often gray, or brown. Their hair may be red, even sandy, or dark in color, perhaps thinning over the years. In many cases they have thin mouths when speaking or smiling, but their lips can also be full.

EMOTIONAL CHARACTERISTICS
ARIES

This is a brave, enthusiastic, imaginative, and energetic person. They are easy to excite and are impulsive, adventurous, in general they are daring. Don't expect this to be a domestic person. They can be hasty, brusque, sharp passionate, and quick-tempered. To the extent that it can be excessive, and perhaps violent.

MENTAL CHARACTERISTICS
ARIES

This is an enterprising, pioneering, confident, ingenious person. Also, scientific, explorative, independent, expedient, precise, progressive and intolerant in religion, aggressive, competitive, and dictatorial. When you have something you want done, give it to this person, no matter how busy they are. They love the challenge.

✮
APRIL - MAY
MEN
TAURUS

Honesty is an important factor with this man, and it's possible that most social formalities will seem dull to him. He may be a frugal spender, but he will acquire the things he desires. He will drive a very good automobile; wear expensive clothes and may treat you lavishly at least in the beginning of your relationship. After the courtship is over however, you will probably see a change in his spending habits as this man does not acquire wealth by spending it. When these men are ready to make love, they want to make love right then, they do not want to discuss it first. Lustful is probably a good word to describe this man. He can be controlled in a manner with the use of affection. As this fellow courts you, It might be a quick bite at a fast food place, or it could dinner be at a very elegant restaurant. You may not know which it will be until you arrive. Possessions mean a great deal to this person. There may be a tendency for this man to smother his mate with his presence, and over protect her as well. After all, she too will become a possession. This is a very independent person, and very set in his ways.

WOMEN
TAURUS
A Taurus woman needs a man who is stable, intelligent and energetic. He needs to be sensitive to her needs and possess a good imagination. He will need good common sense, and be able to provide for her well being. He must understand that this woman requires a financial security. The man who patronizes this woman will not get very far with her. She is much too strong for that.

The man of her choice will never forget a birthday, or an anniversary of any kind. He will cuddle her, comfort her, and compliment her when it is deserved. Will she be a jealous woman, most likely? This is a quiet woman, one who is composed, who seems as if time has no end. However, when she gets into the bedroom she can become another woman entirely. When this woman decides you are her next sexual conquest, don't expect it to be a quick session. To satisfy her needs may take a section of your day. Like all morning, or perhaps all afternoon, or all night. Perhaps all three. A Taurus woman is an artist in several ways. It can be painting, Pen and ink drawings, pottery, sculpting, or whatever, but in bed she is indeed an artist. She likes bedding a man because it feels good and it is a natural thing to do. You will find she likes a man's hands exploring her breasts and she may make them readily available for this purpose. She has the ability to seduce men through many avenues. It could be the low-cut dresses she wears, which allows men to gaze down upon her cleavage, perhaps even a complete view of her breasts. This is a woman who may have breasts so large they cause her physical problems and a few of them consider breast reduction to ease the load they carry. Men rarely tire of watching her hips as she walks because she is good at this kind of seduction as well. Or, is it the way she crosses her legs, or perhaps her bedroom eyes. To respond to this woman, pat her on the butt, kiss her on the neck, and touch her somewhere, anywhere, but somewhere. Perhaps whisper how you would enjoy making love to her in the park after dark, but mean it when you say it, because she will expect it to take place. Also, this is a woman who wants to be a mother.

MARRIAGE
This person needs the solidity of a good sound marriage and that of a good home life. The solidity of marriage shows others that this person is successful at any undertaking, and their self-determination will fight to keep the marriage together. The Taurus is a highly sexually stimulated sign. To the physical extent, that many mates may not last long enough to take care of this individual's needs in the bedroom, and this is in the normal sexual relationship. If, their needs include something outside the normal realm, it can be even harder to cope with.

Some of the problems with having this Sun sign as your mate, are as follows.
If a marriage to this person goes belly up, how do you shed yourself of this mate? You may not be able too without some real effort on your Part. Remember you are a possession to this Sun sign, perhaps even after the divorce is final. If you don't want to be possessed, if not stay away from this Sun sign altogether. It will seem as if they own their mates, and their children. They accept anything being offered, physical, or mental, but don't expect to get anything in return. Remember this is the person who is materialistic in every sense.

NATURAL TENDENCIES

You've heard the story about the bull in the china shop, well the male Taurus is kind of like that when he makes love to a woman. He is an animal and one that can ravage her. Man or woman, the Taurus lover will take much more time to make love to their partners in the bedroom, hours are not unusual. However, as a lover of this sun sign you must also remember you are their lover. You now belong to them, in the bedroom and out. If the lover is married to someone else, they still belong to this lover. If this is someone, who becomes involved in an "Office Affair." The Taurus will most likely help the lover advance in any way they can, for this person often has swaying power in the bedroom and out. This is a person who wants, and enjoys, making love in every position possible, Quite often any place possible as well. Lengthy foreplay may not always be needed, but long lasting love making is of importance. If Venus is in Aries in this lovers chart, no one in their circle, family or friends, is safe from their advances sexually. You will think of this lover as insatiable, and you will find many of these lovers who enjoy hard sex, perhaps in any form. Bondage may be a light form of love making, as it can go much deeper than that. Be sure you know what you are getting into with this lover before you start a sexual relationship. Oral sex may not come to the Taurus lover early, but once they learn how to use it to keep their lover near the edge of a climax, but not going over the top, they will use it to do just that.

SUGGESTIONS TO CONSIDER

Earth signs, Taurus, Virgo and Capricorn are very passionate. Sometimes they can even overpower others. To the extent that other signs may think of them as someone who is a sexual pervert. This kind of attitude, from those who do not understand these sun signs, is erroneous. What one person enjoys sexually may not be enjoyable to everyone else, but that does not mean it's wrong. It only means that those who feel someone is a sexual oddity, is simply ignorant in life's design for happiness, and pleasure. Still, if the two people have the planet Venus in the same sign at the time of birth, their sexual outlook is often the same. This can bring sexual harmony and with this can come sexual contentment. A Taurus with another Taurus can result in hours spent in bed together, neither of them tiring of the fun and games. Though moody, a Cancer will find a Taurus a good lover, and someone who will take command of their lives so they don't have to mess with the details. Virgos' sexual outlook is also a pleasing experience for a Taurus, as are Scorpios, but Scorpios are very strong and may not submit to the ownership of their mate that Taurus feels about their mates. With a Capricorn there is a good chance of happiness.

SPECIAL NOTES

Taurus people are possessive, which means they are possessive of their lovers as well. As a lover, or as a mate, they won't share you in any way without a struggle. This would not be a good sun sign for Aquarians, Libras', Geminis, and perhaps the opposite signs of Leo, Aries, and Sagittarians' as well. The reason for this is that these signs are of a very free thinking group. They cannot be owned or fenced in. To try to impose an ownership restriction on this group will only bring constant rebellion from them. Taurus sun signs enjoy kinky sex, such as being spanked, or having their nipples pinched. Perhaps even some degree of bondage. They are also noisy lovers, to the extent of screaming out loudly during a climax. They also enjoy making love outdoors, and they will masturbate anywhere. The Taurus sun sign also enjoys using the lips and tongue to give pleasure. You should let them. Even while involved in a relationship of any kind with one person, this is someone who can find themselves in bed with someone else as well.

If the planet Venus is found in Aries, and perhaps Taurus at the time of birth, this could be someone who is almost a nymphomaniac in sexual need. They enjoy pornographic materials of any kind, written or visual. Sexual stimulants will also be found close to their bed, such as dildos, perhaps even in their purse.

If you are a Taurus and the lover of a Dual sign, or its opposite sign, such as Gemini / Sagittarius, or Virgo / Pisces, don't expect to be their only lover. Dual signs also means, dual relationships, which will be hard for a Taurus to endure as it gives away control of ownership.

FUNDAMENTALS
TAURUS

The symbol for Taurus is the bull. The bull, as we've all heard about, turned loose in a china shop, brings things crashing down. This is not necessarily true of the human being born under this sun sign. In reality they enjoy the finer things in life, and for the most part treasure them. In fact they are outright possessive of the things they have. This includes their loved ones, wives, husbands, children, lovers, homes, cars, and anything they possess they intend to keep. If they give a gift, no matter who has it, or where it is, it is still theirs. This is because as Taurus is the sun sign controlling the second house of a horoscope and that of personal wealth, even if the object doesn't really belong to them any more they still consider it as theirs. Venus in Taurus in the first house of physical being, may require a lover who can last for a lengthy session of love making. If it is pleasurable to them, they want it to last, and last and last. With this possessive attitude consider the house position Taurus is found on at the time of birth as well. For instance, if Taurus is found on the eleventh house of friends, they will feel they own these people and may not want to share them with others. This is one of the sun signs that produce women with the biggest breasts, especially if it is on the first house of the physical being.

PHYSICAL CHARACTERISTICS
TAURUS

Their head and necks are most often short; with a broad face and perhaps somewhat flat. They have a strong chin and large eyes, dark in color. Their hair is also dark in color, but sometimes they are blond. Sensuous full lips and perhaps a short, sturdy, or plump body.

EMOTIONAL CHARACTERISTICS
TAURUS

Contradictory in emotions, their mood swings make definite statements concerning every emotion possible. These are amorous, artistic, and gentle people. They are also loyal, domestic, and proud. Pay attention to any quick-tempered, or self-indulgent events.

MENTAL CHARACTERISTICS
TAURUS

They are patient, and persistent when pursuing things. They are also thorough, steadfast, conservative, retentive, discriminating, determined, argumentative, stubborn, hasty in their judgments, and materialistic. Often their emotions can control their thoughts.

✯
MAY - JUNE
MEN
GEMINI

A smooth talker, and someone that may try to sweep you off your feet with what seems a vast amount of knowledge. Granted they are smart, but they normally learn a little bit about everything and not a great deal about any one subject in any great depth. Don't misunderstand, this is a very intelligent person and is someone who can con you out of things, all with a glib tongue. Even if you are not ready to give up whatever it is they want. The items they talk you out of may range from the physical to the materialistic items. When you become involved with this person, don't just give them whatever it seems they think they may need, ask for some specifics to be sure they really need it first.

What this man may tell you is one thing, the complete truth may be quite another. This is a mental person and the mind works constantly. New things are always of interest to them, but they will tire of it if it's repeated time and time again. The foreplay to making love may be extensive, often verbally communicated, even of a fantasy nature. All the while their hands may be busy to include sensitive touching.

However, as Gemini is not known as a heavy sexual sun sign, but as more along the lines of a secondary interest, you may want to understand why he wants you, and what are the reasons behind his pursuit.

WOMEN
GEMINI
This woman can make friends anywhere and at anytime, but she will not make a special issue of finding men. The men who approach her will be scrutinized by her carefully. She is suspicious of men who seem to cater to her. Still, she can be good at entertaining men, and several of them all at a time. It's not the quality of men that interests her. It's the quantity of them. As a lover you may seem to be a chosen one day, and then you are out of the running the next. A Gemini woman wants a man who can talk to her for hours, and about anything. Then perhaps, a good time can be had in bed, but soon afterward she will forget all about him until some other time. This is not a woman, who is going to dwell on the subject of love making. Well, a few seem to.

This is a woman many people have trouble keeping up with, as she is always thinking of her next direction in life. She may go on a trip, and upon her return she'll start right where she left off, as if it was just the day before. This woman is gifted with the spoken word, and she can join a conversation of any kind at any time. However, when the conversation starts getting into depth of a particular subject, she is likely to move along to another group discussing yet another topic. It is not that she has gotten bored with the first group, it is because they may have outdistanced her knowledge on the subject at hand. Gemini is an intellectual sun sign, which is to say they learn a great deal about a lot of stuff, but they may not go too deeply into any one avenue of studies to the point that something becomes a religion with them. This is not a woman to confide in with your specific personal problems, as she can be a gossip. If this is the case, your life's issues may get passed along to someone else as a topic of discussions. However, the story as told to her, will have changed so much, that even you may have trouble recognizing the story as having been yours. In sexual matters she will analyze the relationship and wanting to know why she wants this man, or why he wants her. She understands sex very well, but may not actually care from day to day if she needs time in bed with a man. When she does go to bed with a person of interest, she'll want to know what's in it for her?

MARRIAGE

Even if they don't think so, this is a Sun sign that needs to be married. This is a mind that constantly needs nourishment, even if their children need help with their homework, this one has their own studies to deal with. Sexual enjoyment will come after the mental studies have taken place. Yet, this is a continual student, and some think of Gemini as a cold Sun sign. The mind does not seem to shut down long enough to enjoy a sexual encounter. Anyone who seems slow may be an irritation to this person, to the point that this person may even become cranky and quite annoyed with those close to them. Okay, or maybe even anybody close by.

Some of the problems with having this Sun sign as your mate, are as follows.

This Sun sign is similar, in a sense, to that of a Scorpio. This sign may make more out of a conversation than is really there. It's as if they think there is something written between the lines that does not exist. There is no sense in giving this person a reprimand for making a mistake, as they themselves don't have any idea how it happened.

You must keep this Sun sign busy in a marriage. If not, they will become bored, and you don't want this person as a bored mate and one who seeks a new experience. If this person, as a mate of yours, seem to travel a great deal, perhaps gone for days at a time, you might want to consider that perhaps there is another family with the same last name as your own living somewhere along the traveled path.

If you are contemplating a divorce from a Gemini, watch out for the checks written on your bank account. Did you really write them, or were they written for you, and of course your signature will appear on the checks.

NATURAL TENDENCIES

Though I have told you that Gemini is a dual sign and prone to enjoying either sex as a partner, this is not necessarily the case. It will depend mostly on the sign that Venus is in at the time of birth, and the natal house position of Venus. More often than not, sexual interest in the same sex is not the case, perhaps some curiosity may linger in their minds but acting out those thoughts will not take place. Geminis' often marry young, sometimes just to seem normal, sometimes for the new experience, and many times a marriage can fall apart because they acted to quickly in their decision on the mate they've chosen. When traveling away from home, and those that know them, a Gemini can feel the excitement building as they consider taking a lover, probably just for a short time while they are on the road. In their early years they may not seek out oral sex, it is only when they come to understand it as a tool to give sexual pleasure to their sexual partner, whoever that may be, that they show some interest in this form of love making.

The Gemini woman can rival the Taurus woman in outlasting their lovers. If, at the time of birth Venus was in Aries, then the Gemini would be more daring, and perhaps more forward in seeking someone to play with. If Venus was in Taurus, then the Gemini will be more inclined to seek someone who will make them suffer in some manner as though thoughts of masochistic tendencies seem to linger in their minds. These feelings are intensified if Venus is found in the first house of the physical body, because when it is here it demands sexual satisfaction. Venus in the first house promotes addiction of some kind. Often one addiction is replaced by another.

SUGGESTIONS TO CONSIDER

It has been said that the air signs, Gemini, Libra and Aquarius can get along with anyone, and basically this is true. However, when they choose a mate as an air sign they are seldom true to each other, mainly because the relationship is, in a sense, tame. Still, if the two people have the planet Venus in the same sign at the time of birth, their sexual outlook is often the same. This can bring sexual harmony and with this can come sexual contentment. As with the other air signs, a Gemini should do well with the fire signs. Aries will make the Gemini toe the line. Leo can be a lover who springs a situation for making love that surprises a Gemini, but also brings a curiosity about performing sexually in the manner that Leo proposes. Gemini will find Sagittarians' an ideal lover. Still, it might be a good idea to remember that these are dual signs and any kind of sexual play might unfold. Perhaps it can involve more than the two of them.

If you are a Gemini and not of a highly sexual nature, it is recommended that you stay out of long term relationships with those born between October and March, as this is the time frame when Venus is in the sun signs noted for addiction of any kind. Sexual addiction is not unlike any other kind of mind altering drug and if you can't keep up with the persons sexual needs, you will find the relationship failing. If you like to experiment that is okay, but don't make a long term commitment until you are certain the relationship will work out to your satisfaction. You should also be sure you are capable of fulfilling their needs as well. You do not have to heed the recommended sun signs for each group you find listed here in this book, but history tells us it is best.

SPECIAL NOTES

As a general rule Geminis have enough trouble with their sexual identity. Sometimes they learn early in life that they are different from most other sun signs in this respect. They enjoy sex, but not in great quantities. Sometimes a part of the problem may stem from the fact that they don't know which sexual partner they really want, will it be male, or female. Will it be one person, or two, or even more? Will they be promiscuous, probably? And all at the same time. One thing they do learn is how to please the opposite sex. They enjoy oral sex, and become very good at giving their partners a sexual high in this manner. They can be great lovers, and they are not above using sex as a tool, often making their bed mates feel as if they are the best they've ever had. Then as soon as it is over, their mind quickly goes to something, or someone of more interest. The love making that just took place now long forgotten. They do like making love outdoors, not quite exposed to prying eyes, but nearly so. If they become sexually hungry and don't have a lover nearby, they will masturbate.

Because Gemini is a communicative sun sign pornographic stories will bring about a quick need for a climax, as this is a sun sign that enjoys the written word. Even while involved in a relationship, of any kind, this is someone who can find themselves in bed with someone else.

FUNDAMENTALS
GEMINI

This is an intellectual person. They are well aware of most things going on, and they may use this knowledge to their own benefit. Other than Sagittarius, the opposite sign to Gemini, this is one of the best people to have in the sales department of any business. This is someone who can talk you into, or out of most anything. If you know them personally, you must become aware of when they are telling you what you want to hear. I say this because sometimes they tell the truth, just not all of it. Experimentation may be a fun thing for them to try, and with Venus in Gemini in the first house they will no doubt have multiple lovers, and of course either sex, perhaps all waiting in line at the same time. All dual signs exhibit this kind of behavior. This would include, Sagittarius, Pisces, and Virgo is often considered a triple sign. As the ruler of the third house of communication, this is a person who wants to talk, it can be any subject, but you should make it interesting. One other thing here, Gemini is one of the sun signs who like to feel hands on their bodies, and they enjoy putting their hands on others. This is a touchy feely person and sexual desires are often brought into play in this manner.

PHYSICAL CHARACTERISTICS
GEMINI

This is someone with a long head and neck. They may have a broad forehead and a pointed chin. Their eyes will be expressive, their hair light in color; a small mouths with thin lips accompanied by an aquiline nose. Their long fingers will remind you of a pianist, and their body will be slender. Perhaps widening with age.

EMOTIONAL CHARACTERISTICS
GEMINI

It seems they lack concentration, and tend to be insensitive, but will seem charismatic. They enjoy short distance travels, and are not known for being domestic. They make good company and their conversations are changeable as well as interesting. They can seem to be cold, or lacking in affection, as well as unsympathetic. When angered they will be genial, but quick-tempered, and ungrateful.

MENTAL CHARACTERISTICS
GEMINI

Skillful in manual expressions, and inventive when needed. This is a versatile person, one who is adaptable, self-expressive, very curious, but superficial thinkers. They may appear as they are sometimes scatterbrained, or tricky.

✸
JUNE - JULY
MEN
CANCER

This is a real homebody, and someone that will ask to take you to his place to cook dinner for you. Let him. Odds are you will enjoy it, but domesticity is the key word here. A lot of women like this man simply because he thinks in a romantic manner. Although he can become someone, who tends to smother his partners with too much affection. This man is not one for going out to dinner a great deal. Though when he does go out to dinner, he knows where the best places are, and at the best prices as well. The home and the family are utmost in this man's mind. He makes a commitment to a relationship, and one of dedication to a lasting union. In the event there is a snag in the love affair he will continue to try working things out as long as his partner is similarly dedicated. To be unfaithful to this man is to create a great wrong and doing so can be costly to the guilty party.

This can be a moody man. You will find this out as the weather turns, when it is warm and sunny outside, he will be in good humor. If it is cloudy, foggy, rainy or similar weather, he can be moody and down. This man will have gone through many different problems in his lifetime often not attaining the real treasures of life until his later years. Still he is someone who will fully understand the problems of others.

WOMEN
CANCER

As a man, you will find this woman wants you to proceed at a slow pace with her, as she does not like to be rushed. She will insist that she is the only one in your life and without this condition in place a man will not keep her long. She may seem to be a weak woman, but this is not the case. She will seek a man who can take complete care of her, emotionally, and financially. When she has the right male in her life, her sexual appetite will be open to nearly any avenue of exploration as long as it is just the two of you. You will find she likes a man's hands exploring her breasts and she may make them readily available for this purpose. She is also a woman who may have large breasts, often to the point of physical discomfort. Once you have an established relationship with a Cancer Sun sign woman, you can make love to this woman from the front, back, top or bottom, and she is open to oral, and possibly anal sex. She also likes making love anywhere it might be wet. Such as showers, outside in the rain, on the beach, in a pond, you name it. However, she does like romantic settings so you should use them. Such as candles, a fire in the fireplace, silk sheets on the bed, champagne and anything else along these lines. She will not tolerate a rough man or a man who treats women harshly, as this is a sensitive woman. She prefers a man who will take the initiative, but once aroused she can easily take the lead.

The man in her life will have to understand her
moods because she will have them, probably
forever. It will be an understanding that he cannot
ask her what is wrong because odds are she
won't know herself. This woman will make a
commitment to a relationship with lasting
dedication, and to be unfaithful to this person is a
mistake.

MARRIAGE

This is the natural homemaker. Someone who feels the need to have a home life, and will work hard at making it come true. This is a very romantically, imaginative, and an emotional person. When it comes to their love life, this is one of the more faithful Sun signs of the Zodiac. Even though this is the natural homemaker, they can miss the true love boat until later in life. One other factor with this sun sign, they are often found in interracial relationships.

Some of the problems with having this Sun sign as your mate are as follows.

A negative side would be the possibility of continual nagging, a common event with this sun sign. They are highly emotional and cannot take criticism. If you offer constant criticism to this mate, the marriage will fail. If the marriage begins to fail, the Cancer Sun sign may become greedy, holding onto everything, and everyone. The point is, can the current marital mate handle it. You have never experienced a bad temper, until, you are set upon by an angry Cancer Sun sign. You cannot escape the crushing crab's claw, and they know if anger does not work, tears will. However, if this is your mate, expect him, or her to work at keeping the relationship together. It matters not whether it is good for either of you.

NATURAL TENDENCIES

This is a sign that embraces sensitive issues. Their feelings are easily hurt, and they have difficulty with any kind of rejection, or criticism, good or bad. To the extent that they are in love with the idea of love itself. Cancer people can be aggressive in sexual situations as long as they feel they are wanted. If they feel they are just being used, or not enjoyed, you might as well throw them into a cold shower. It will have the same affect on them. If they are bedded by someone who is a noisy lover, and one who reaches a climax noisily, one who's hands and feet jump around during the love making, one who moans and groans as if in great enjoyment, then this lover will inhabit the Cancer's mind for years to come. Cancer sun signs, and perhaps those with a Cancer personality, will enjoy sex and a lot of it with a lot of different people. This is the homebody, the person who wants a home and wants to make love at home. They are natural cooks and may want to cook a meal for their lover in the beginning of the relationship, or wining and dining. Such as the, "Candy is dandy, but liquor is quicker," attitude. The Cancer sun sign can be found entertaining possible lovers who are older than themselves, in fact this is a common trait. This is also someone who will become involved in relationships with different ethnic groups. The women may have big breasts and when they are self confident they will gladly show them off to the opposite sex through the use of low-cut blouses so their cleavage can be seen.

SUGGESTIONS TO CONSIDER

The water signs, Cancer, Scorpio and Pisces, are a very emotional group pf people. They may find it difficult to express themselves on a sexual basis. Especially if coupled with another water sign. Still, if the two people have the planet Venus in the same sign at the time of birth, their sexual outlook is often the same. This can bring sexual harmony and with this can come sexual contentment. One of the things lovers of this sun sign find, is that their highly emotional nature can bring about a session of love making that is memorable. One not soon forgotten.

This sun sign needs a way to get their sexual needs fulfilled, even if it takes place with self gratification. Their emotional nature makes them a natural for the sun sign of Taurus. The body of a Cancer sun sign likes to be felt physically so the hands of a Virgo are often very welcome as well. An ideal mate may be found with a Capricorn as they like the passionate pursuit of a Cancer.

If you are not of a highly sexual nature it is recommended that you stay out of relationships with those born between October and March, as this is the time frame
when Venus is in the sun signs noted for addiction of any kind. Sexual addiction is not unlike any other kind of mind-altering drug and if you can't keep up with the persons sexual needs, you will find the relationship failing. If you experiment, that is okay, but don't make a long term commitment

until you are certain the relationship will work out to your satisfaction. You should also be sure you are capable of fulfilling their needs as well. You do not have to heed the recommended sun signs for each group you find listed here in this book, but history tells us it is best.

SPECIAL NOTES

These are emotional people, and this shows up in bed, or wherever it is they are found to be making love. Lying out in the open is a great stimulosus for this person. They do masturbate but they would much rather have someone taking care of them sexually than to have to take it upon themselves to reach a climax. They do enjoy oral sex and will bestow it upon their partners at unexcepted times. Though this is generally a one person at a time lover, it is also possible that this can be a promiscuous lover. Even while involved in a relationship of any kind, as this is someone who can find themselves in bed with someone else.

If you are a Cancer and though it will pain you as a lover of a Dual sign, or one of its opposite signs, such as Gemini / Sagittarius, or Virgo / Pisces, you shouldn't expect to be their only lover. Dual signs also mean, dual relationships. Cancer sun signs may be someone who can become involved in incestuous relationships, even if it is not them who starts them along this path.

FUNDAMENTALS
CANCER

Cancer's symbolism is that of the crab and if you remember how crabs walk, which you'll recall is sideways. When you think of this, and are speaking to someone born in this sun sign, remember that when you ask them a question, especially if it is something of a personal nature, you will find they sidestep the question. Most likely will sneak out of answering your question by asking a question of their own. This is another sun sign that produces women with big breasts, especially if it is on the first house of physical being. This is an emotional sign, and wherever this sign is found on the chart, emotions about that part of life will be apparent. If it is on the fifth house of children, this will be one of the most emotional parents to be found. Cancer rules the fourth house of 'Home.' So, when you are dealing with one of these people you know they are drawn to the life of being at home. The title, 'Homebody,' fits this person. When you have time to spend with this person you may find they keep company with any and every, ethnic race in the world.

PHYSICAL CHARACTERISTICS
CANCER
A large head, round like that of the moon and sitting on top of a short neck with large eyes, and a short snub of a nose. Their mouth will be large with full lips. Large breasts are common, and they fight weight control for most of their lives. Their hands and feet are small, and they walk in such a manner as to seem labored.

EMOTIONAL CHARACTERISTICS
CANCER
An artistic and dreamy person, as their mind may be held in a maternal role whether they want to be or not. This is someone who may possess a psychic, and imaginative nature. They are calm, but restless in nature, sometimes lazy and self-indulgent. Their moodiness surpasses every other sun sign.

MENTAL CHARACTERISTICS
CANCER
Very versatile, self-sacrificing, and receptive to others. They express great adoration for their ancestry and thorough, and determined in their pursuits. They may seem to be cautious, reserved, brooding with constantly changing moods, even somewhat negative.

✮
JULY - AUGUST
MEN
LEO

Here is the true family man, the one who believes in having children and spending a great deal of quality time with them. This is also a very out going man and one who will buy you gifts in his attempts too win your affections. You may not feel indebted to him for his generosity, but that will be one of his methods of winning you. This is the man who wants quality things in his life for show and tell. As a potential mate, you may become one of those prized items. He will treat you well and give you material possessions, but you may be one of his. You may find it tough to stay on the pedestal upon which he may place you, and he seems blind to the fact you could fall off this high perch. This is one of the more handsome looking signs of the zodiac, and he is an independent individual. As a lover of this man it may take some time to develop, but you should become aware of his inner being, as this sun sign can hide their true nature.

WOMEN
LEO

This woman talks a good story, but she often lacks the ability to perform as good as she lets others believe. She likes her sex, that and her love life will generally be intertwined together. However, it can happen that in her life this will not always be the case. Usually she is a devoted wife, until, or unless things in her life are falling apart. There is no question this is an attractive woman and she knows she has an impact on men. She enjoys being in the limelight and will look for a man who treats her like a queen. This would be a man who heaps praise upon her, and buys her jewelry. If you wish to pursue this woman, you better not be a cheapskate.

If you become this woman's lover, and if you are a good lover, this woman can become a wildcat in bed. She enjoys oral sex, she likes to be on top, and she may enjoy pornographic films and stories. She will treat the man in her life with visual views of her in flimsy night wear, or you may just as easily find her completely nude. This is the natural exhibitionist so nudity is an enjoyable state to her. This, could be a woman who quickly opens her legs to a man's view as he is passing by her car and as she opens the door. Will she be wearing underwear, maybe, maybe not? As a man, you must understand that this woman enjoys foreplay, perhaps more than the act of making love itself.

MARRIAGE

As the ruler of the fifth house of love, Leos' fall in love easily. Not necessarily wisely, or fortunately, but easily. It seems as if it is nature's wish that the Sun sign Leo should be joined with a mate, and this Sun sign dislikes being alone. They want someone to shine for, and as a result, they often place their mates on pedestals. Though it can devastate them when their chosen mate actually falls off the pedestal, and becomes a regular human being. You know, someone with faults.

Some of the problems with having this Sun sign as your mate, are as follows.
As the mate to this sign you will not mind getting the gifts they bestow upon you. The Leo Sun sign gives gifts to those they fancy as their's, or want as their's. However, will you, as their mate, put up with the gifts they give to others. If you are deeply involved with a Leo sun sign, you will need to constantly bolster this person's ego, it is expected of you. Will you love them, no question, at least until it ends.

NATURAL TENDENCIES

This is someone who wants to be seen and will dress expecting to be noticed for what they are wearing. It might be the best in clothing, or the female might display herself in a truly dazzling attire for the evening. This can include a very see through negligee. They can overdo themselves to the extent that they burn out in their early years. When this happens, they may turn to other sexual variations to attempt sexual fulfilment. This could be perversions like masochism, sadism, and Leo's have an affinity for children, so this could be a problem with them as well. It is the emotional release from sexual need that fuels this person. If charm won't get them into bed with the one they are pursuing, perhaps gifts will do the trick. When they are younger, they may fumble a lot in their attempts at love making. This then makes them practice all that much more to get it down right, as they want to be perfect. The preferred bed mate will be one who is charming, witty, graceful and intelligent. They will often shy away from lovers who seem to like kinky sex because they enjoy the good old fashioned normal sexual routine. The women of this sun sign are among the best of liars. They can tell a falsehood like no one else and still convince people that it is true.

SUGGESTIONS TO CONSIDER

The fire signs, Leo, Aries, and Sagittarius are exceedingly passionate, but when they mate with other fire signs there is a constant ongoing battle for supremacy. The clash among them will usually drive them apart. Still, if the two people have the planet Venus in the same sign at the time of birth, their sexual outlook is often the same. This can bring sexual harmony and with this can come sexual contentment. Leo's coupled with an air sign may have to exert some self control. The way an air sign lights the fires of a Leo can lead to early climaxes. This is not a problem for the female of the sign, but it can be a problem for the male. Sometimes a male can consider masturbating before hand so that he can last longer when the love making with an air sign actually begins. Leos' being a show-and-tell person, will enjoy the natural grace and charm of a Libra. An Aquarian brings a very satisfactory physical union to both the Leo and the Aquarian.

If you are not of a highly sexual nature it is recommended that you stay out of relationships with those born between October and March, as this is the time frame when Venus is in the sun signs noted for addiction of any kind.

Sexual addiction is not unlike any other kind of mind-altering drug and if you can't keep up with the persons sexual needs, you will find the relationship failing. If you experiment, that is okay, but don't make a long term commitment until you are certain the relationship will work out to your satisfaction. You should also be sure you are capable of fulfilling their needs as well. You do not have to heed the recommended sun signs for each group you find listed here in this book, but history tells us it is best.

SPECIAL NOTES

Leo sun signs will indulge in what some may call 'Kinky' sex. However, it may not be a very involved kind of kinky sexual activity. As the lover with Leo this is someone who likes the missionary method and likes being the one on top. They also prefer monogamous relationships to love affairs, but are not beyond them. Leos' may also enjoy oral sex and are noisy lovers. The men like pornographic magazines while the women like the written word of sexual fiction. This is a person who likes being seen naked. To the point that they may flash their private parts to others, or just accidentally allow themselves to be seen in some manner. It turns them on sexually.

If, as a Leo and the lover of a Dual sign, or its opposite sign, such as Gemini / Sagittarius, or Virgo / Pisces, don't expect to be their only lover. Dual signs also mean, dual relationships. This is someone who can become involved in incestuous relationships, even if it is not them who starts them along this path.

FUNDAMENTALS
LEO

Leo the lion is the ruler of the kingdom, just ask them. This is the sunshine and that is what this person wants to do, is to shine. Whatever planet is found in this sign, it too will want to outshine any other planet in this chart. This is someone who wants to be at the center of attention, and so does its opposite sign, Aquarius. In charts the Sun represents men and so this sign is one of masculinity. This sign does produce some of the more attractive people as does the opposite sign of Aquarius. Wherever this sign appears on the chart, that person will shine in that area. As Leo rules the fifth house, the house of children, they are often very fond of children.

PHYSICAL CHARACTERISTICS
LEO
Wide faces and sometimes flat, curly hair often light in color. As with the other fire signs, Leos' are inclined to frontal baldness. Their self image may bring the tendency to combing their hair in a comb-over style. They have large mouths and commanding eyes. Their physical bodies are well formed.

EMOTIONAL CHARACTERISTICS
LEO
Faithful in most relationships, rich in their emotional life, and affectionate to everyone in their group or family. This is a proud and idealistic person, one who is chivalrous, and likes the domestic life. They can make more out of a situation than is true, which can lead to illusions, this is also someone who can sometimes be cruel.

MENTAL CHARACTERISTICS
LEO
Mentally generous, ambitious, and self-sacrificing. In bad times they are optimistic, even though they may seem fixed in their opinion they can be magnanimous in dealing with others. They are opposed to secrecy, and seem oblivious to animosity. This is a challenging, and bold person. They can be domineering, and bigoted.

✳

AUGUST - SEPTEMBER
MEN
VIRGO

This man may actually pursue you for your
intellect. He himself will be an intellectual and a
learned person. He can also be very much the
critic, the one who will criticize your faults trying to
make you better whether you want to be or not.
Something most people do not take easily, but
praise will also come forth for your better qualities.
Most often this is the person who is overly neat
and meticulous in every way, and the perfect
gentleman. There will be trips to the museums,
libraries, or other places of knowledge. He may
also have some tendency toward personal health
conditions, which could lead to being someone
who suffers from hypochondria.

When he finds out what it is you like in a lover, he
will try to become the best lover you have ever
experienced. If you want variety, you will need to
convey this message to this man as a lover. For
him fantasy will cause excitement. Such as an
invitation to take a shower with you. If you agree
to this bathing with him, you should know he is
also being sure you are clean. I'm sorry, but this
goes back to his fear of infection, and possible
hypochondria. It may seem as though he wants to
wash you, but there will more to it than that. He
will delight in feeling every part of you in his soapy
hands. His imagination can cover many sexual
situations for you to enjoy and he will enjoy them

as well. There are those who think of these men as cold in bed, and there are those who think this is one of the best of lovers. There could be some unusual conditions in this man's love life. Marriage itself, may not be an important factor in his life.

WOMEN
VIRGO

This, is a woman who will look for a man whom she can help, or to benefit him in any way she can. This is the perfect woman, if you doubt this, just ask her. This is not someone who will start a relationship with just any man, as she will take her time to find the perfect lover for herself. Though her passions may take awhile to burst into flames, the potential lover just has to wait for the event to take place. She will insist on being perfect in her lovemaking whatever manner that may be. She will learn everything about the man of her choice so she can fill every need he may have. All she needs is to find the time to do these things. When she falls in love, it will be a deep love, a lasting love. If you bathe with this woman, you will find her washing you. It may be because she wants to be sure you are clean, but it may also be because she likes to feel you grow in her soapy hands.

This is a woman who will enjoy a man who spanks her on the ass or explores her everywhere with his hands. She does have a drawback, which is the fact she seems to be a magnet for the wrong kind of men. Men who are restrictive to her in some manner, though she may subconsciously seek these men out to fulfill her need to take care of them.

MARRIAGE

If you are chosen by this Sun sign as a life's mate, odds are you really are in it for the long haul. As this Sun sign rarely marries until they are sure they have chosen wisely. This is not someone to jump into marriage hastily. This may not be an overly exciting sun sign, but they will be a very faithful mate. This can be someone who grumbles and criticizes more than they give praise. Though a Virgo is supposedly a neatness freak, this is not always the case. They can also be quite careless and very untidy.

Some of the problems with having this Sun sign as your mate, are as follows.
Do not expect this to be a doting parent as children can get on some Virgo Sun signs nerves. Children can just be too untidy, too messy, or too noisy, etc. You may wonder why they have children when they want to just put them in a corner somewhere. If your marital position is deteriorating while you are married to a Virgoan, do not think it will be an easy path to travel. It won't be. This person can make your life a living hell. You've never heard real criticisms until you are on the bad side of this Sun sign. You will hear complaints that you never realized needed attention until you begin having problems while married to a Virgo. Before you agree to wed this sign, be sure you understand their sexual desires, and the gender they prefer.

NATURAL TENDENCIES

It may seem odd, but Virgos' are virginal in many ways. Though you might not think of it as it happens to you, still when you find them inviting you to bathe with them it may sink into your mind as to what is going on. Virgos' find it sexually stimulating to bathe with their lovers, they like the hands on feeling as they wash their sexual partners private parts, but the basic side of this, and it may be only mentally or psychologically in nature, but it is simply the fact they want that person to be clean. A Virgo is an earth sign and in many ways exhibits the pull of Saturn in their lives. This leads them to relationships where they are the older lovers, one who teaches the younger sexual partner the things that are needed in successful love making. As a youth they may seek older lovers to learn the art of love making, and as they age they will seek the younger lovers to teach those same artful methods. These are often big spenders, even if they can't afford to spend the money, and it might not be their money they are spending. This is a person who learns all about sex and its secrets, this doesn't mean they will try all of them for the experience, but they know about them. Virgos' are often found to be a dominating lover, or the one who wants to be dominated.

SUGGESTIONS TO CONSIDER

Earth signs, Taurus, Virgo and Capricorn are very passionate. Sometimes they tend to sexually overpower others. To the extent that other signs may think of them as someone who can be a sexual pervert. This kind of attitude from those who do not understand this sun signs, is erroneous. What one person enjoys sexually may not be enjoyable to another, but that does not mean it's wrong. It only means that those who feel someone is a sexual oddity, are simply ignorant in life's design for happiness, and pleasure. Still, if the two people have the planet Venus in the same sign at the time of birth, their sexual outlook is often the same. This can bring sexual harmony and with this can come sexual contentment. When you start making love with a Virgo, don't be bashful, start feeling them as soon as it seems appropriate. Explore their body with your hands and I mean all of their body. When coupled with a Taurus, a Virgo will find they have similar sexual appetites. It will not be what some purists think of as 'Normal.' They get along well with a Capricorn, but may find a Pisces a very delightful lover.

If you are not of a highly sexual nature it is recommended that you stay out of relationships with those born between October and March, as this is the time frame when Venus is in the sun signs noted for addiction of any kind. Sexual addiction is not unlike any other kind of mind-altering drug and if you can't keep up with the persons sexual needs, you will find the relationship failing. If you experiment, that is okay, but don't make a long term commitment until you are certain the relationship will work out to your satisfaction. You should also be sure you are capable of fulfilling their needs as well. You do not have to heed the recommended sun signs for each group you find listed here in this book, but history tells us it is best.

SPECIAL NOTES

Virgos' are indeed the kind who enjoys kinky sex. Why, you might ask, simply because it is different from the norm and thus exciting to them. They will masturbate, but perhaps not as much as most other sun signs. They will have sexual toys ready for use if, and when they decide to use them. When they do make love, they like to do so in the afternoon. They prefer a monogamous relationship, but can be talked into any kind of relationship. Virgos enjoy the use of their hands to explore a lover, and at any time. You would not think of Virgos' as a person who likes to be touched, but they do. They also enjoy potential lovers to feel and explore them with their hands. The right kind of hand exploration of the Virgo's body can stir the sexual need. Ask them where and how they enjoy this kind of foreplay after you have started doing this hands on love making. Don't be surprised to find out they may like some harsh treatment.

If you are a Virgo, you may also be aware of how the dual signs, or their opposite signs, such as Gemini / Sagittarius, or Virgo / Pisces, can enjoy dual relationships.

FUNDAMENTALS
VIRGO

Virgo is known as the sun sign of the Virgin, well don't bet on that being the case.

This is a mind with constant analysis taking place. Wherever this sun sign is found, the thinking process is found. Virgos' can analyze things to death. Self criticism is also a key part of this sun sign, and that self criticism will take place in whatever natal house this sign is in, and any planet found in this sign at birth will be one of learning. This is the realm of the intellect. Any planet found here is also scrutinized. Neatness and cleanliness are also a way of life, well most of the time. As an example of this you will find that someone who has Venus, the planet of love in Virgo at birth, they will want to wash their lover in the shower, or bathtub. Not only to examine them, but to be sure they are clean. Venus in Virgo also enjoys a constant learning experiences. Virgo rules the sixth house, which is sometimes a restrictive house so planets found there may also be somewhat restricted.

PHYSICAL CHARACTERISTICS
VIRGO

Pronounced forehead, their faces may have noses with wide nostrils. Their mouths are small, but with well-shaped lips. They can have wide shoulders and long arms and legs. This is a sun sign that holds its beauty for most of their life. This is someone who is a hands on individual, their hands on you, and your hands on them, it suits them well.

EMOTIONAL CHARACTERISTICS
VIRGO

Kindly, and humane, a highly evolved type who lives to serve mankind without thought of self. This is a domestic person, and can occasional become melancholy. This is also someone who can be untrustworthy in little things. This is the perfectionist so any untruthful conversation will seldom be found out. They can be petty, or fussy even superficial in affairs of the heart.

MENTAL CHARACTERISTICS
VIRGO

This is an ingenious, witty, studious, and a skillful person. One who is versatile, introspective, scientific, and methodical. This is the skeptic who is critical of everything. This can be the hypochondriac, one who fears disease and poverty. Things they do may have ulterior motives behind them.

✫

SEPTEMBER - OCTOBER
MEN
LIBRA

This person is interested in the arts, and any art form he may possess along these lines will be evident in his life style. He may also dress in the latest fashion, or he could just as easily be very sloppy in his appearance. The problem you will encounter with this male is that as a lover, or partner of any kind, you will often have to make the decisions as to which stage play you might like to see, or too chose which of the fine restaurants at which you would like to dine. This fellow will have trouble making up his mind about many things, which shirts to wear, which tie will go with the shirt that ultimately gets chosen. What time to leave, should he get gas for the car now, or wait until after he picks you up.

Though in the beginning of your relationship you may not be aware of it, he has trouble making decisions. When he does make up his mind on most matters it can seem as if it is done with difficulty. After you get to know him if you question his decision it could throw everything into mental disarray. He is a quiet person, but he does enjoy social affairs. To entice this man, try a subtle perfume and satin sheets. However, don't be surprised by the inventiveness of love situations you may encounter when with him.

Before you allow yourself to get deeply involved with this man, you should understand what it is he expects from you as a lover. Sometimes his idea of the perfect lover is a bit lofty. In reality the Libra male will not consider sex the most important thing in their lives. Peace and harmony could be.

WOMEN
LIBRA

This is a classy lady in the bedroom, or out. She likes men to be well informed and she can hold her own in a good conversation. She often finds herself interested in older men, intelligent men, and men of good taste. This is not a woman that just any man is going to get into bed. This woman takes more than just some sweet talk. It may take several things, or perhaps it may involve very little, but it will take something. Perhaps a dinner for two, an evening at the theater, a good wine by the fireplace, or maybe just a good conversation. This woman does not expect to open her own doors, the man in her life is expected to do that for her, and he better be well groomed. Being dressed sloppily and taking her to a neighborhood bar is not going to work well to entice her. Spoil her with gifts and she will spoil you. This is an attractive woman, she may not be a raving beauty, but men will notice her.

Though this is not someone who lives for sex, she exudes it in her walking and mannerisms. She has hips that are provocative as she moves, and she smells good. As a girl the Libra may have been misunderstood, some thought she was flirting, where in reality she was seeking an admirer. Once you have her in bed, you can use sexually explicit language, and a mirror over the bed will be welcome.

MARRIAGE

The problem of making up their mind extends into the marital relationship as well. This Sun sign takes a long time to choose a mate, so long that most of us would tire of the extended search. Because of their idealistic feelings about marriage, theirs should last. They have little interest in trying different partners. This is not a Sun sign to create waves in their lives, they don't want to face the aftermath caused by problems anyone creates. They tend to see the world through rose colored glasses and are in love with 'Love,' itself.

Some of the problems with having this Sun sign as your mate, are as follows. You may find yourself making many of the decisions for this person, well maybe not all of them, but at least the important ones. And get used to having others do stuff for them, even if you had gotten around to it, it is their nature to have others do things for them. No, they won't have to ask, it will be just be understood.

NATURAL TENDENCIES

Libra's learn every aspect about sex. One way or another. They can become the sexually hottest lover of all. They understand sex for what it is, what is considered Kinky and what is not. They simply love being in bed with a lover and going at it to the extent that every avenue of love making has been explored, and tested for its sexual value. Variety with Libra's is often the real spice of their sex life. Libra women are real women. That is to say this is the woman who grows her garden and then cans the preserves for future use. Much like the women of old who planned on preparing for the worst of times. She may be wearing a six gun on her hip, dressed in a flowery print dress, while barefooted in a country field, and still look like a woman men want to take to bed. They can tend to place their mates on pedestals, still accepting the fact that they may fall off that lofty perch. Libra's are different in that they find love, then learn to enjoy sex. Whereas most other signs learn to enjoy sex, then learn about love. They are attracted to the opposite sex who is self-confident and can show off without being conceited, or arrogant about doing so. The men want a woman who looks like a woman, and the women want men who look like men.

SUGGESTIONS TO CONSIDER

It has been said that the air signs, Gemini, Libra and Aquarius can get along with anyone, and basically this is true. However, when they choose a mate as an air sign they are seldom true to each other, mainly because the relationship is, in a sense, tame. Still, if the two people have the planet Venus in the same sign at the time of birth, their sexual outlook is often the same. This can bring sexual harmony and with this can come sexual contentment. Libras ' are an interesting group as lovers. They have a side to their nature that goes unnotched. On one hand they can seem demure, quiet with a charming disposition, and at the same time have a sexual nature that will surprise many potential lovers. The fire signs are good for a Libra, as they need the leadership and drive supplied by the aggressiveness of the fire signs.

If you are of this sun sign and not of a highly sexual nature it is recommended that you stay out of relationships with those born between October and March, as this is the time frame when Venus is in the sun signs noted for addiction of any kind. Sexual addiction is not unlike any other kind of mind-altering drug and if you can't keep up with the persons sexual needs, you will find the relationship failing. If you experiment, that is okay, but don't make a long term commitment until you are certain the relationship will work out to your satisfaction. You should also be sure you are capable of fulfilling their needs as well. You do not have to heed the recommended sun signs for each group you find listed here in this book, but history tells us it is best.

SPECIAL NOTES

This sun sign can enjoy kinky sex when it is not over the top. Other than that this is a pretty straight sexual person. If as a Libra and a lover of a Dual sign, or its opposite sign, such as Gemini / Sagittarius, or Virgo / Pisces, don't expect to be their only lover. Dual signs also mean, dual relationships. I've been advised by a Libra that bisexuality was of interest as well. You may find Libra women dressed in lingerie and the men wearing only a Tee shirt.

FUNDAMENTALS
LIBRA

Libra is depicted in symbolism as the scales of justice. But this is not really the case. In reality it indicates someone who tries to balance things out in life. The constant looking at one side of things to make sure it balances with the other side and it drains their decision making. It will seem as if they simply cannot make up their minds. Which is often true? Venus in Libra in the first house may have trouble choosing which new outfit to buy, or which lover to wear it for. This is the person, who when he or she says. "Do you mind if I get comfortable?" It may be into something slinky, or it could be nude. Ether way it is done to entice you into thinking the same way they are thinking, unless they change their mind. This is an artist, but art is found taking place in many forms that may not be recognized as an art.

 Perhaps a welder who makes the best welds to be found, to him this is an art form. A chiropractor's hands are his art form. A painters hands are his art form. A musician's hands are his art form, and the list goes on and on.

PHYSICAL CHARACTERISTICS
LIBRA

Their facial features are often small and regular with good teeth. Their mouth and chin are well formed, not large, not small. Their hair is fine and on the women it is often found to be long. With bodies well proportioned, they may seem like they tend to being hippy, perhaps heavier in middle life.

EMOTIONAL CHARACTERISTICS
LIBRA

Sometimes they harbor secrets about loves lost. This is someone who is charming, sophisticated, and a romantic. In any endeavor they choose to enter they are enthusiastic, but their minds are changeable. This is a person who may not be artistic, but knows art.

MENTAL CHARACTERISTICS
LIBRA

Libra's tactful abilities can often persuade others of what needs to get done. Their decisions, though hard to come by, are normally approved of by those involved. This is a person who loves to dabble in things, be it art, or gardening. Any project they have found an interest in lately. In a sense they are materialistic, but not so you would notice. They are good at helping others in decision making because they won't take sides with the other parties involved.

✭

OCTOBER - NOVEMBER
MEN
SCORPIO

This man will want to know all about you. Even if you don't want him too. The questions he asks may be subtle in nature, but continuous. You may not be aware of it while he inquires about you, but he will provide you with very little information about himself. He feels as though you might hold an advantage over him if he gives away personal information. He does not want anyone to know him too well. He will take you to a cozy little hideaway for the weekend, or perhaps to isolated beaches. Those quiet out of the way places can provide fond memories for him, as he enjoys the quiet solitude. This can be an intense lover. Some think of him as oversexed, perhaps even unconventional. But sexually his own satisfaction could be a problem. Jealousy could be in abundance with this man as well. Mood swings may take place, and you will never know why. But you will be left with the feeling it is your fault, whether it is your fault or not.

WOMEN
SCORPIO

Whatever this woman does for her mate, she will expect to get something in return. At some point the man in her life will have to pay for her services one way or another. As a mate to this woman, you will never know her fully because she keeps personal secrets about herself wholly unto her. Normally she becomes her mate's right hand, and she does this to protect her own future. A weak male will not fare well with this strong woman, as a weak male will not be able to keep up with her demands. However, the myth of the Scorpio woman can be just that, a myth. This is not always a heavily sexed sign though it is thought of in that manners, still it can in fact it can be quiet the opposite. She does however, control the sexual portion of her life and may use it to her advantage. Whatever that may be. If jealousy on her part enters her life, you as the recipient, may not even be aware of her method of getting even with your indiscretions until a later date. It won't leave you in a comfortable position. After all, you wounded her pride.

MARRIAGE

They say this sign is a highly sexual oriented sign. In some cases this is perhaps true, but don't depend on it. Yet, if you are one of those chosen by this Sun sign as a mate, expect them to be with you through thick or thin. In fact this person may be with you even if the marriage is over with, they just don't realize it's finished.

Some of the problems with having this Sun sign as your mate, are as follows.

You will never have a secret from this person. Somehow, they will find out anything they want to know, and they want to know everything about you, or anyone connected with you, and everyone else for that matter. This Sun sign is similar to that of Taurus, in that it is possessive. If the marriage goes on the rocks, this person does not want to give it up. If you wrong this Sun sign while married, you will come to understand the word, 'Revenge.' Oh, you may not be divorced, but you will wish you were. You will suffer while still married even if it is done quietly. Did this person marry you for your money?
Are you sure? Were you aware of their jealous streak before you got married?

NATURAL TENDENCIES

Scorpios who have Venus in the sign of Scorpio will have a problem with fulfilling their sexual needs. Venus in Scorpio can produce a high sexual appetite, almost to the point of Nymphomania. If this planet should fall into their first house, their sexual drive can be closer to an ongoing addition. This is a condition they live with their entire lives, and it is on their mind constantly. This person may want to consider the sun signs born between October and March. It is these sun signs that may have similar sexual needs. During these months Venus can be found in Aries, which will be aggressive in the search for sexual mate who can keep up with them. Venus in Capricorn is a social sexual need, that is this may be someone who wants to make love to everyone in their social circle. Aquarius is also someone who wants to love everyone, and may try to do so.

SUGGESTIONS TO CONSIDER

The water signs, Cancer, Scorpio and Pisces, are a very emotional group pf people. They may find it difficult to express themselves on a sexual basis. Often two water signs together may bump heads as they both ride a different emotional roller coaster. Still, if the two people have the planet Venus in the same sign at the time of birth, their sexual outlook is often the same. This can bring sexual harmony and with this can come sexual contentment. A Taurus will find a Scorpio very satisfying, especially one who has Venus in the sign of Scorpio at birth. Taurus has the lasting ability and Scorpio has the need. Scorpio with Venus in Scorpio will find a Capricorn with Venus in Capricorn, a natural mate. Both with a heavy sexual need, and both able to provide the fulfillment for that need.

If you are a highly sexual person you may want to consider those born between October and March as this is the time of the year when Venus is in the sun signs noted for addiction of any kind. Sexual addiction is not unlike any other kind of mind-altering drug. If you find someone to your liking don't make a long term commitment until you are certain the relationship will work out to your satisfaction. You should also be sure you are capable of fulfilling their needs as well. You do not have to heed the recommended sun signs for each group you find listed here in this book, but history tells us it is best.

SPECIAL NOTES

Scorpio sun signs often enjoy what some may call 'Kinky' sex. To a Scorpio it will be perfectly normal. This may only be oral sex, or simply the enjoyment of pornographic materials. During love making this is someone who likes being the one on top, or in control. Depending on where the planet Venus is found in the natal chart, and the sign it was in at the time of birth, this could be a highly sexual person. This is one of the sun signs that can fall into a group who become addicted to sex. Making love outside is often a welcome diversion as well. Do they masturbate? Yes they do as sexual fulfillment is not easily attained. Even while involved in a relationship of any kind, this is someone who can find themselves in bed with someone else. It has been found that this person may be a lover who can enjoy anal sex as well, but don't take this for granted.

If you are a Scorpio and the lover of a Dual sign, or its opposite sign, such as Gemini / Sagittarius, or Virgo / Pisces, don't expect to be their only lover. Dual signs also mean, dual relationships.

FUNDAMENTALS
SCORPIO

Scorpios are very secretive, especially about themselves, yet probing when it comes to others. The curiosity about others is to the point where nothing is sacred, or private. If you make this person angry, even if it is only them that think this way, they will enjoy some sort of revenge. Scorpio seems to carry a lot of influence, but is it because they know so much about everybody that they get their way. They seem to have an influence on how things turn out in the end, in a sense, the death of things. Whoever has Venus in this sign tends to over indulge in anything that catches their interests. Whether it is sex, drugs, art, music, or whatever. Scorpio rules the eighth house and this is the basic house of sex and sexual organs.

PHYSICAL CHARACTERISTICS
SCORPIO

They tend to having small faces with deep-set eyes and heavy brows. Their mouths are not large, and most often they have small, thin lips. They normally maintain a small, slender body for most of their lives. A dark complexion is common as well.

EMOTIONAL CHARACTERISTICS
SCORPIO

This is an emotional person, one who may not make it known openly, but if you spend time with these people you will know when they are in a funky mood. They don't have to tell you with words. If you wrong this person you will encounter an impersonal and often revengeful individual. If their mates get involved with another person sexually, they may not allow a divorce to take place, they would rather have you close at hand to punish anyway they choose. Their imagination can make them suspicious of most anything. They don't pretend to be domestic.

MENTAL CHARACTERISTICS
SCORPIO

It is natural for this sun sign to investigate things, they seem to need to know the secrets of everything and everybody. They are smart with a penetrating intellectual way about them.

✭

NOVEMBER - DECEMBER
MEN
SAGITTARIUS

Here is the sports fan. A very outgoing man, but when you are traveling in his company you will be found at football games, at the basketball court, perhaps sailing, on ski trips, or any of the other many sporting events. This is someone who takes chances which can show up in any number of ways. Gambling of some kind could be an issue with this person, and at the same time he can be a very theological minded man as well. He enjoys the home life and entertaining friends and associates in the home. Even then, when the sporting games are on, he will be in the den watching them on television, perhaps his male friends will be there also. If he flirts with other women, odds are they won't be serious as he doesn't want to truly endanger his marriage. This is also one of the best liars you may ever meet so you may never know how true he is to you.

Promiscuity with this person takes place in many forms, and this man may exercise some of them. If you experience anger coming from this person during any part of your relationship, analyze your relationship carefully before any long-term commitments are made. As a lover he will take what comes naturally at the time, whatever that may be.

WOMEN
SAGITTARIUS
To love this woman, is to love a challenge, and to keep her to yourself is equally a task. Her independence requires that her lovers, or mates, give her unquestionable freedom. This woman and the Aquarian, are two Sun signs that are not like other women. They can fall in love, and deeply, but it is not unusual for them to keep sex and love as separate parts of their lives. If you have been a lover of one of these women, you will know how lucky you have been, and to have had her once, is to remember it forever.

If you want to know this woman very well, you better like the out of doors. Should you just want to chat with her, expect to do so at some kind of sporting event. To get to know her around the office can be hard to do, as she is a ball of fire and energy. To tie her down long enough to make a connection is a trying matter, and if your want to know what she thinks of you, all you need do is ask. Be aware however as sometimes the truth can be brutal. If she wants you, odds are you will know it before the actual conquest takes place. She can be ready to make love in a very short time; in fact, she is ready nearly anytime. Once you are in this woman's life don't try to fence her in. If you attempt to control her by fencing her in, you will find yourself with an empty corral.

To approach this woman you need to be direct. Don't beat around the bush with her, and if you are a weak male, you won't get to the bedroom with her. You have to be strong, but do not confuse strength with that of a cave man, because this is not the kind of strength she looks for in a partner.

MARRIAGE

This is not someone who likens to marriage easily. Its like putting ice cream into a hot oven and expecting it to stay frozen, it will not happen. Once married, it will be an unusual event for the Sagittarian to stray from the marital bed. Oh, it can happen, but this is someone who is concerned with what others think of them, which may be what keeps them on the straight and narrow. A Sagittarian is a good liar, and they can spot one easily, and if you think this is an uneducated person, think again.

Some of the problems with having this Sun sign as your mate, are as follows.

This is someone who needs to be free. Though they do marry, they are at a constant battle with the opposite sex. As a single person this is a Sun sign that can wander from bed to bed if their mate is of a narrow mind, or restrictive. They may do this just to see if they can win the game. They will try to get away with nearly everything they do that seems to be wrong by the rest of us, and most of the time they do.

NATURAL TENDENCIES

Despite the fact that this sign is known for wandering, they do not do this as a rule. When they have chosen a mate, it is often for life. Still when they are out and about their eyes are still selecting their next bedroom partner for the night. It may not happen, but they still look and consider the potential of being with someone different. Sagittarians begin early in life to masturbate and continue doing so for most of their lives. Though a seemingly self confident person, when disaster strikes, or serious problems, this is a person who can go to pieces quickly. Perhaps the largest fault with a Sagittarian is the tendency to gamble. It does not matter what the sport is, and it may not even be a sport they bet on, but it will be on something of chance. Anger can be directed toward those close at hand, even in marriage. If you encounter one of those who have a problem with anger, perhaps you should avoid any involvement that will place you in jeopardy.

SUGGESTIONS TO CONSIDER

The fire signs, Aries, Leo and Sagittarius are exceedingly passionate, but when they mate with other fire signs there is a constant ongoing battle for supremacy. The clash among them will usually drive them apart. Still, if the two people have the planet Venus in the same sign at the time of birth, their sexual outlook is often the same. This can bring sexual harmony and with this can come sexual contentment. Sagittarians are not known to get involved in odd sexual behavior. They like the old fashioned normal love making to their liking. Gemini is a good mate, and Libra can disturb the normalcy of Sagittarius by suggesting something of a variety, and if done correctly, it will be enjoyable to both of them. Though Aquarius is more often than not a good mate for a Sagittarius, if the Aquarian has Venus in Capricorn at the time of birth, it can bring about a sexual relationship that is often more than the Sagittarius can handle.

If you are not of a highly sexual nature it is recommended that you stay out of relationships with those born between October and March, as this is the time frame when Venus is in the sun signs noted for addiction of any kind. Sexual addiction is not unlike any other kind of mind-altering drug and if you can't keep up with the persons sexual needs, you will find the relationship failing. If you experiment, that is okay, but don't make a long term commitment until you are certain the relationship will work out to your satisfaction.

You should also be sure you are capable of fulfilling their needs as well. You do not have to heed the recommended sun signs for each group you find listed here in this book, but history tells us it is best.

SPECIAL NOTES

As a dual sun sign promiscuous behavior can be a common factor with this sun sign. It is the very nature of dual signs to behave this way. Most often when they are in the company of a lover in a public place, you will never see the connection between the two of them. They will enjoy kinky sex but only after it has been introduced to them, and even then it may take some time for them to open up to this form of love making. Oral sex can also be something they will come to enjoy. It has been found that this person may be a lover who can enjoy anal sex as well, but don't take this for granted. This too, may not be a quick conversion from the normal sexual behavior. They may turn into noisy lovers after they experience the enjoyment of letting go of the primal sounds when climaxing. Making love outside in the afternoon is also something they like to do. Talking sexually to them and using blunt language can turn them on. Even while involved in a relationship, of any kind, this is someone who can find themselves in bed with someone else. Also, though this is a dual sign they may not be aware that Geminis', Virgos' and Pisces are also dual signs and may have more than one lover at the same time, and not necessarily of the same sex.

FUNDAMENTALS
SAGITTARIUS

This is another dual sign, and this may be one of the best liars you will ever meet. They will often have more than one lover, married or not. This sun sign, or even if it is found on the ascendant, may be tough on their lovers. If not physically, then mentally. This is someone who likes to gamble, it could be anything that they gamble on, as long as it has chance involved. To some degree you will find this same condition takes place with the opposite sign, Gemini as well. Sagittarius is the traveler, the roamer, one who is never satisfied to stay in the same place. Other than Gemini, this is the natural sales person, but normally they are involved in large sales, or sales of large things.

PHYSICAL CHARACTERISTICS
SAGITTARIUS
With a high well rounded forehead, there is a
tendency to hair loss over time. A long nose is
offset by a large mouth with full lips. They may be
a bit on the hippy side, but this is not normally
noticed as to the long legs. Their hair can be
anything from dark blond to auburn in color. They
may be inclined to stoop.

EMOTIONAL CHARACTERISTICS
SAGITTARIUS
They can be impersonal in their emotions, or
seemingly so in public. They are daring, impatient
and self indulgent. Often open hearted and
pleasant to be around.

MENTAL CHARACTERISTICS
SAGITTARIUS
This is a smart person, one who is philosophical
and conscientious. Normally in a good mood, and
curious. Professionally they are extremely
ambitious, often in a financial manner. They get
hunches, and for the most part, should pay
attention to those hunches. However, they must
learn the difference between hunches and wishes.
Gambling can be a problem as they are fearless
when it comes to taking chances.

✮
DECEMBER - JANUARY
MEN
CAPRICORN

This is a very social man and someone who can become deeply involved in the business community. This man may well have his own business, or be in a favored position in a business. A position that perhaps requires a social indulgence on his part. It should not come as a surprise to find him contemplating a career in the political field. He normally has a great sense of humor, and an easy manner about him. This is also a down to earth person, one who thinks things through logically. He can at times seem somewhat boring depending on the company around him at the time. He prefers long term relationships in his life, the term, "One night stand," usually will not apply here. But, long term love interests may be a factor in his life. Don't be afraid of being the leader in pursuing a romance with this person as it is acceptable.

This is not known for being a strong sexual sign, but if Venus is in Capricorn, or Aquarius at the time of this person's birth, he can exhibit very strong, and lustful desires.

If you are in a relationship with this man and it starts to deteriorate, do not expect to hold it together with sex, sex alone will not work.

The men, and women, of this sun sign are prone to seek those who are younger, or even older than themselves. It seems as if ten years difference between their ages works out well.

WOMEN
CAPRICORN

This is a woman whom under the right circumstances can shed a mate without so much as a backward glance. This won't happen often in their life, but it can happen. She can easily live a solitary lifestyle, but would rather not. The older she gets the more sexually appealing she can be. As a child she is often the tomboy and the result is that she may have been overlooked as a real girl. It's as if the boys did not take her seriously, as to her feminine side. She is also a daddy's girl. Yet, as an adult she can be more of a feminine woman than many other females. Don't mistake this woman as "Just a woman," this woman is a schemer, a doer, and she will be successful in her chosen direction in life. It might be as a business CEO, or running a business of her own. She is the one who is thinking professionally when others around her are merely plodding along. She can be shy, and will be a very devoted lover when love is found. She can choose the wrong mate in that she may choose losers, but if someone takes an unfair advantage of her, it will not be forgotten. This woman is the one who suggests to the man she has chosen, that perhaps. "We should get together sometime." Yet, this is exactly what she means. When she finds out what, the man in her life likes about a woman, be it legs, breasts, hips, long hair, or whatever, she will dress in such a manner as to enhance that part of herself. She is drawn to older men because she feels they know how to treat a woman, but she will not give of herself easily. What she finds attractive is a man who has old-fashioned values, with a touch of class, and the ways of a gentleman. This is not known for being a strong sexual sign, but if Venus is in Capricorn, or Aquarius at the time of birth, this woman may exhibit very strong and lustful desires. The men, and women, of this sun sign are prone to seek those who are younger, or older than themselves. It seems as if ten years' differences between their age's works out well.

MARRIAGE

This Sun sign may be too busy in their daily lives to stray from the marital bed, in fact perhaps too busy to spend much time in it with the chosen spouse either. This is the politician, no matter what the platform may be. The Sun sign of Capricorn is not known as a lustful sign, but Venus in this sign is another matter. This person can talk to the opposite sex, about sex, with little self-consciousness; it is after all, a topic of mutual interest. This Sun sign may be too busy to get things done for you, and perhaps they may seem to be a cold person.

Some of the problems with having this Sun sign as your mate are as follows.

Be careful in choosing this sigh as your mate, and be sure what they prefer, man or woman. When in a good marriage with a Capricorn, if you stray from the marital bed it will not be forgotten, or forgiven. Did I say they wouldn't stray from the marital bed? No, I did not. The sense of humor is inviting, but it invites everyone. Often, their invitation includes you letting them come into the privacy of your home. Or, was that the bedroom.

NATURAL TENDENCIES

Capricorns who have Venus in the signs of Aquarius or Capricorn, and in the first house of their natal chart are well aware of their ongoing sexual needs. If this planet should fall into their first house, their sexual drive can be closer to addition. Venus in Capricorn is a social sexual need that is this may be someone who wants to make love to everyone in their social circle. Okay, maybe even a wider circle than that. This is a condition they live with their entire lives, and it is on their mind constantly. Capricorn is a sun sign that may use sex as a tool to get what they want. They use people in much the same manner. Capricorn loves to be seduced. If you are someone who is interested pursuing a Capricorn, don't be shy. Tell them what you want.

This person may want to consider the sun signs born between October and March. These sun signs may have similar sexual needs. During these months Venus can be found in Aries, which will be aggressive in the search for sexual mate who can keep up with them. Venus in Scorpio can produce a high sexual appetite, almost to the point of Nymphomania. Aquarius is also someone who wants to love everyone, and may try to do so.

SUGGESTIONS TO CONSIDER

Earth signs, Taurus, Virgo and Capricorn are all very passionate. Sometimes they can overpower others. To the extent that other signs may think of them as someone who can be a sexual pervert. This kind of attitude from those who do not understand these sun signs, is erroneous. What one person enjoys sexually may not be enjoyable to another, but that does not mean it's wrong. It only means that those who feel someone is a sexual oddity, are simply ignorant in life's design for happiness, and pleasure. Still, if the two people have the planet Venus in the same sign at the time of birth, their sexual outlook is often the same. This can bring sexual harmony and with this can come sexual contentment. Capricorns get along well with the signs of Taurus and Virgo. Scorpios and Pisces may also make good lovers for this sign.

If you are a highly sexual person you may want to consider those born between October and March as this is the time of the year when Venus is in the sun signs noted for addiction of any kind. Sexual addiction is not unlike any other kind of mind-altering drug. If you find someone to your liking don't make a long term commitment until you are certain the relationship will work out to your satisfaction. You should also be sure you are capable of fulfilling their needs as well. You do not have to heed the recommended sun signs for each group you find listed here in this book, but history tells us it is best.

SPECIAL NOTES

Capricorns enjoy being the lover on top when making love in the missionary style, and they are noisy lovers. This is one sun sign that really enjoys oral sex, giving and getting the attention in this manner. They may also use sex as a tool to get what they want from a mate.

FUNDAMENTALS
CAPRICORN

This is the charmer and someone who uses people, or uses their personality to woo people. They have a great sense of humor, but can come across as cold and calculating. This is a person who should be in business for themselves, even if this sign is found on the ascendant, it will be a business-minded person. This is also a social thief, the one who takes paper clips, pens and paper home from the office, even if they are not needed. Kleptomania is often found with this person, and this is the person who thinks of kidnaping as a business venture. Venus in this sign is often show up as an addiction problem of some kind. If Venus is found in the first house as well, this could be a very charming sexual predator, but generally of their own age group.

PHYSICAL CHARACTERISTICS
CAPRICORN

A high forehead with piercing eyes. A long nose can be accentuated by the thin lips of the mouth. A Narrow chin does not help to offset the rest of the face. Often found to be large boned individuals, and with large hands and feet.

EMOTIONAL CHARACTERISTICS
CAPRICORN

Not someone to take chances, they often become inhibited. If rejected by others, they can turn upon themselves. A feeling of. "It must be my fault." Can bring on self pity, which in turn will make them unforgiving and easily irritated. Often their mind may fall in love with something, or someone, without clearly thinking the reasons through.

MENTAL CHARACTERISTICS
CAPRICORN

This is a powerful mind, one that focuses on the direction of interests. Once they have found a belief in something, their opinion becomes fixed. This is the diplomat, the politician, someone who learns how to use others to get what they want. Literature and science are directions of interest. This is an optimistic humanitarian.

SPECIAL NOTES FOR ALL SUN SIGNS

In my discussions with those who enjoy bondage, I found, to my surprise, that the fantasies they favor, or prefer to read about, involve submission. One of the more prominent reasons for the need to be submissive is often because they themselves are domineering, or controlling individuals in their normal daily lives. Being submissive removes their personal control, and gives their lovers the manipulative power. A role reversal that they enjoy as they are placed at the mercy of someone else.

The thought of being ravished by their lover with no control on their part, other than an agreement of how far to go, is the sexual high. In some cases reaching a climax without this kind of love making can be difficult. The planets most often involved in this kind of sexual nature are Saturn, Mars, Venus and the luminary representing their gender.

That is the Moon for women, and the Sun for men. Often that luminary planet can be found in the twelfth house at the time of birth. The sixth house could be involved, but it is not as restrictive as the twelfth house. The restriction on the planets in these houses can bring difficulty in obtaining the desired goal. The closer to the ascendant, the more powerful the influence.

Kinky sex. You need to look at the aspect relationship between Venus and Mars, Saturn, Neptune and Pluto. You may want to keep handcuffs, soft rope, Dildos, or other items around that this lover enjoys. The Sun, representing men, or, the Moon representing women, may be located in the twelfth house, but this is not always the case.

HOW AND WHERE TO MEET THE PEOPLE OF YOUR CHOICE

How you meet people is quite often left to chance, but that doesn't have to be the way it's done. You can control it most of the time. Often people think that if they go out to nightclubs, bars, taverns and the like, that is where people go to meet. And, they do, but not the ones who are looking for long term relationships. You need to think about the things that interest the individual, and where these things will take place, and that is where you go to meet them. I'll list some of the basic items for you as to each of the twelve sun signs, and you can figure out where these will take place in your community, or, as nearby as you can find.

AQUARIUS

Aquarians enjoy air shows, nautical events, aircraft and art museums. As well as live theater, and the people who are found in those circles. If you have live theater in your area try to make some contacts where you can get invited to auditions, or cast parties. Perhaps find out where they go after the night's performances are over.

They also enjoy sailing and flying aircraft. With this in mind you will want to spend time at small airports, or marinas. Sailing may be one of the easiest ways to get involved in this group. You could volunteer as crew member on a race boat and you can learn about this activity at most marina offices.

Astrology is another favored interest, so if there is a book store that caters to this group you can inquire about the things going on here. However, you must remember that this kind of group can lead to several offshoots, such as witches covens, seances and any number of similar interests.

They also have an interest in birds, so perhaps a bird watching group in your area can offer an outing to you. This is an inventive group of people, and they enjoy exploration. Stonework and masonry are also things of interest to these people. If you want to get to know them better, invite them to something that is unusual.

Perhaps to a show at the planetarium, a 'Fly in,' at a nearby airport, a live theater stage play. Just not the normal run of the mill stuff you can do every day. Even you can just invite one of them to sit at the end of an outgoing runway at the airport to watch the planes come and go.

PISCES

These people can be found in several odd groups, though it will only seem odd to those who are unaccustomed to their interests. This is one of those groups who are similar to the Aquarians in that they are also found at similar places.

Pisces are interested in witch's covens and seances as Pisces are intuitive people and find these groups of interest, and they often have some psychic ability of their own. They enjoy the surroundings at Abbeys, convents, monasteries and hermitages. They also like clandestineness of secret societies, as well as spies and spy networks. None of which may be easily found.

They also like Astrology and the occult worlds. Sailing is another of their interests and could be an easy way to get involved in this group. You will find these are the fishermen and can be found at public docks with a fishing pole in their hands.

Occasionally you may find it easier to meet a Pisces at a fishing event being sponsored by a local club or sportsman's shop. You could inquire as to bait shops along the waterfront if any events are scheduled in the near future and perhaps volunteer to help out. This way you will be in the center of the event and can meet people easily.

You should also be aware that there are a good many women who are avid fisher people. Most water events will have Pisces people around them, such as swimming pools and swimming events. They like poetry, writing and you may be able to locate a writer's group where you can meet these kinds of people, or find a reading that is going to take place at your local library. They also like fantasies and alcohol. You might explore the idea of sharing a fantasy with them over a glass of decent wine, perhaps a fantasy that includes them. Who knows where it might lead. Try taking them to the Aquarium, or walks on the beach. If you can arrange it, take them swimming in the nude.

ARIES

You have to embrace the idea of some danger to get involved with this group, as they are adventurous in this manner. Adrenalin rushes are a common factor in their lives and it comes in many forms. These are the soldiers, policemen, firemen or the like. Although it is not always the things that take energy that will lead to their whereabouts. These are woodcarvers, welders, pioneers and chess players. You may look into a local group of wood carvers, or perhaps a chess club to find someone who interests you. Look for the person who wears something red, and hats are commonly worn by these people. This is someone you'll invite to the nearby dirt race tract. Power boat racing, sky diving if you can handle it yourself. Perhaps a local wrestling match, anything with some element of danger.

TAURUS

Taurus people enjoy the arts, to include live theater, and the people who are found in those circles. If you have live theater in your area try to make some contacts where you can get invited to auditions, or cast parties. Perhaps find out where they go after a night's performances are over. Art exhibits, art studios, and museums. Perhaps piano recitals will expose you to this group as well. Or, perhaps a choir somewhere in your area as they like singing and musicals.

This is someone you'll take to the museum, or art gallery. If you go to dinner, don't expect to go cheap, a fast food restaurant will not impress them.

GEMINI

Anything having to do with travel, or communication is where you will find these folks. You might look around bookstores and libraries. You could ease into a conversation in the reading room as an early form of communication with someone from this group. If you have access to a school, you will find these are the teachers, and librarians. They also like to walk so perhaps a group that gets together for a daily walk. Writer's groups also draw this kind of mind into its group. When you meet this person, have your gift of gab ready, short humorous stories will go over well. If you have a knowledge of an unusual nature, ask if they would like to learn something about your world. You could try taking them to somewhere where authors give readings of their work, or perhaps poetry. When you are comfortable, tell the stories of sexual fantasy, yes you can make them up. If not, try finding a book on adult bedtime stories.

CANCER

This is the homemaker, the person who likes food and cooking. It might be tough to make an acquaintance in this group if you are not part of a neighborhood where you can make a connection. You might find them around the water, as they like fishing, fountains, lakes, and water related sports. They are often found in the world of real-estate, or as storekeepers. They also enjoy swimming and water occupations. If you can cook, and when you meet someone like this, offer to fix them dinner, and have a good wine. If you are in their home and shared a meal make it a point to help pick up the table and to do the dishes, don't wait to be asked. If you can arrange a tour at a bakery of any kind, take this person along. Perhaps a 'Home and Garden show,' will help you solidify your new relationship. If you happen across a family reunion at a public park, check out the people who are doing the cooking and serving, who knows, you might find someone to your liking.

LEO

These are passionate people. Passionate about whatever it is they are doing, or who they are with. They like card games, and can be found gambling at roulette tables. You will find them organizing family picnics or events in the park. They like social events, such as playing golf, going to shows for the entertainment of the old fashion stage play. If you are at a resort, you'll find this person around the fireplace. They will come across as arrogant, but they do get involved in love affairs, though not often. If you are at someone's home, look for them out on the porch, or around kids. If you have a good Zoo nearby, invite this person to go with you and be sure you take them to see the large cats. Or, if you are at the zoo, look for them near these same cages as they are fascinated by these large felines. Taking them to an art gallery would also welcome as would a good show at the theater.

VIRGO

This is someone who will have small animals as pets, cats and dogs. This would be a good way to open a conversation with a Virgo. This is a mental person so you'll find them in professions that require thinking. Such as clerical work, civil service jobs, or something that requires a craftsman.

Veterinarians or teachers are common areas for this person to be found, but anything with detailed work involved. You may find them at the library, if not in the reading room area, try behind the counter. When you meet this person, you better be dressed in clean clothes, do not speak roughly, and don't lie. Anything you can take them to that involves mental thinking. This is a person who is a hands on type. So, if you caress them gently with your hands, it will often be accepted, and enjoyed. But don't start our being over friendly in this way.

LIBRA

This will be the person at social gatherings who seems very charming and using diplomacy when it is required. One way to spot them in a crowd is to look for the person with wide hips, or hips that undulate with an easy movement. This is an artist, and it will not be of any particular art form. You'll find them in parts of the country where the air is purest. They enjoy music, paintings, pianos, poetry, and oddly, jugglers. If you know of some event that contains one or more of these things taking place, make an invitation to take them along. Live theater is always popular with this person as they enjoy actors and actresses. This is an affectionate individual, and they like the bedroom. No matter whose it is.

SCORPIO

This is not someone you will get to know easily, you see they don't open up and divulge much about themselves to anyone. This will be the quiet one, but the one who is asking questions of others and getting the answers, even though it may seem subtle. They do like animals, but generally small ones. Out of curiosity they also like the intrigue and mystery found on headstones in the cemetery. This is the detective kind of person, one who reads mysteries and stories of espionage. Irritate them and listen to the sarcasm that comes from them.

To get to know someone with this group you'll have to put some effort into doing so. This could be a profession that includes detective work, perhaps a chemist, or secrets of any kind.

SAGITTARIUS

They can be found around areas where there are large animals, or hiking areas. These are your explorers and those who find education a must. They enjoy literature, philosophy, politics, and to some extent, morality. Often they will be deeply involved in theological beliefs, and teaching. An occupation may include legal practices, perhaps an attorney, or even a court clerk. If you are involved with a group who travels much, or a traveler yourself no matter whether if is by land or sea, you will come in contact with this group. So, where to meet them can become a problem. Court houses, horse back riding stables, your local travel agency as well as churches and colleges. Perhaps even in a local marathon of some sort. They can also be found at race tracts and casinos as they like to gamble, still you should keep in mind that if you meet them here, they will leave their money here as well.

CAPRICORN

You might find a Capricorn any where from an Abbey, to the Antarctic Ocean. They also like old things, or things that may hold secrets. Such as basements, cellars, cemeteries, old churches, clocks, convents, tombs, and dungeons. While you are browsing at an antique store perhaps, you can strike up a conversation with someone else who might be there. This is someone who gets involved in the political side of life and that of government service. Their natural charm opens doors for them and they know how to use this personal ability. You'll find this is often the owner of a business, not necessarily a large business, but one that requires a hands on owner. If you think you've met a Capricorn, ask them what they like to collect, because odds are they collect something.

SECTION TWO - PERSONALITIES

In section one you learned about the individual nature of people, this section will explain how you can determine their personality as well. Let me explain the difference between the two of them and how they come into play in life. The individualism is determined by the birth date, the personality is determined by the hour of their birth. Often the individual part of their nature is modified by the personality, and does not fit the normal description of their sun sign that you read about. At this point you need to read both the sun signs for the Individuality and the sun sign for the personality. This will give you a pretty clear idea of the person you are researching and concerned with.

A simple example of this might flow as follows. Let's say a man is born as an Aries. Now Aries is a sign of aggression, or a great deal of self assertion in whatever path they decide to follow. This is the sign of the fireman, policeman, or soldier. One who enjoys danger to some extent. However if he is born about six o'clock in the evening, he would have the personality of a Libra. This ascending sign could make him docile and potentially someone who does not like disharmony. Someone who is more into the arts rather than that of a warlike attitude. You will often see both of these, the individualism and personality traits, in every person you meet. In this case he could still be a policeman, but doing the job of something like that of a hostage negotiator.

The personality is commonly developed about the age of five to seven years of age. It happens at that time because as children we are allowed at those ages to play and mix with other children. As we all know and understand children are not always kind in their treatment of others who come into their neighborhood realm. It is because of this fact that, as the new kid on the block, you put up a false front. A front that seems to protect you, at least to some degree. It is a false front that the others accept, and this false front is your life long personality. The sun sign that shows up on your first house cusp is that of your personality.

I'll explain to you how to find out what a persons personality is by using a simple chart that you can adapt for any person, and born at any time of day. Below you will find six charts. In the right-hand time column of chart four, 8:00 To 10:00 PM, you will find that an Aries born between those time frames will have a Libra ascending sign, which is the personality. At this point you read both sun sign information portions of section one. It will be the Personality that you may see as the most familiar part of the person, but not always.

PERSONALITY CHARTS

The birth times used here are for the fixed even hour time periods. However, Odds are they will still provide the correct ascending sign with a birth time of an hour plus or minus factor on either side of the hours listed in these charts.

Chart One

Signs	Time	Pers.	Signs	Time	Pers.
6:00 To 8:00 AM			8:00 To 10:00 AM		
Aquar	↕	Aquar	Aquar	↕	Pis
Pis	↕	Pis	Pis	↕	Aries
Aries	↕	Aries	Aries	↕	Tau
Tau	↕	Tau	Tau	↕	Gem
Gem	↕	Gem	Gem	↕	Can
Can	↕	Can	Can	↕	Leo
Leo	↕	Leo	Leo	↕	Vir
Vir	↕	Vir	Vir	↕	Lib
Lib	↕	Lib	Lib	↕	Sco
Sco	↕	Sco	Sco	↕	Sag
Sag	↕	Sag	Sag	↕	Cap
Cap	↕	Cap	Cap	↕	Aquar

145

The birth times used here are for the fixed even hour time periods. However, Odds are they will still provide the correct ascending sign with a birth time of an hour plus or minus factor on either side of the hours listed in these charts.

Chart Two

Signs	Time	Pers.	Signs	Time	Pers.
10:00 AM To 12:00 PM - Noon			12:00 Noon To 2:00 PM		
Aquar	↕	Aries	Aquar	↕	Tau
Pis	↕	Tau	Pis	↕	Gem
Aries	↕	Gem	Aries	↕	Can
Tau	↕	Can	Tau	↕	Leo
Gem	↕	Leo	Gem	↕	Vir
Can	↕	Vir	Can	↕	Lib
Leo	↕	Lib	Leo	↕	Sco
Vir	↕	Sco	Vir	↕	Sag
Lib	↕	Sag	Lib	↕	Cap
Sco	↕	Cap	Sco	↕	Aquar
Sag	↕	Aquar	Sag	↕	Pis
Cap	↕	Pis	Cap	↕	Aries

The birth times used here are for the fixed even hour time periods. However, Odds are they will still provide the correct ascending sign with a birth time of an hour plus or minus factor on either side of the hours listed in these charts.

Chart Three

Signs	Time	Pers.	Signs	Time	Pers.
2:00 To 4:00 PM			4:00 To 6:00 PM		
Aquar	↕	Gem	Aquar	↕	Can
Pis	↕	Can	Pis	↕	Leo
Aries	↕	Leo	Aries	↕	Vir
Tau	↕	Vir	Tau	↕	Lib
Gem	↕	Lib	Gem	↕	Sco
Can	↕	Sco	Can	↕	Sag
Leo	↕	Sag	Leo	↕	Cap
Vir	↕	Cap	Vir	↕	Aquar
Lib	↕	Aquar	Lib	↕	Pis
Sco	↕	Pis	Sco	↕	Aries
Sag	↕	Aries	Sag	↕	Tau
Cap	↕	Tau	Cap	↕	Gem

The birth times used here are for the fixed even hour time periods. However, Odds are they will still provide the correct ascending sign with a birth time of an hour plus or minus factor on either side of the hours listed in these charts.

Chart Four

Signs	Time	Pers.	Signs	Time	Pers.
6:00 To 8:00 PM			8:00 To 10:00 PM		
Aquar	↕	Leo	Aquar	↕	Vir
Pis	↕	Vir	Pis	↕	Lib
Aries	↕	Lib	Aries	↕	Sco
Tau	↕	Sco	Tau	↕	Sag
Gem	↕	Sag	Gem	↕	Cap
Can	↕	Cap	Can	↕	Aquar
Leo	↕	Aquar	Leo	↕	Pis
Vir	↕	Pis	Vir	↕	Aries
Lib	↕	Aries	Lib	↕	Tau
Sco	↕	Tau	Sco	↕	Gem
Sag	↕	Gem	Sag	↕	Can
Cap	↕	Can	Cap	↕	Leo

The birth times used here are for the fixed even hour time periods. However, Odds are they will still provide the correct ascending sign with a birth time of an hour plus or minus factor on either side of the hours listed in these charts.

Chart Five

Signs	Time	Pers.	Signs	Time	Pers.
10:00 PM To 12:00 AM - Mid Night			Mid Night 12:00 AM To 2:00 AM		
Aquar	↕	Lib	Aquar	↕	Sco
Pis	↕	Sco	Pis	↕	Sag
Aries	↕	Sag	Aries	↕	Cap
Tau	↕	Cap	Tau	↕	Aquar
Gem	↕	Aquar	Gem	↕	Pis
Can	↕	Pis	Can	↕	Aries
Leo	↕	Aries	Leo	↕	Tau
Vir	↕	Tau	Vir	↕	Gem
Lib	↕	Gem	Lib	↕	Can
Sco	↕	Can	Sco	↕	Leo
Sag	↕	Leo	Sag	↕	Vir
Cap	↕	Vir	Cap	↕	Lib

149

The birth times used here are for the fixed even hour time periods. However, Odds are they will still provide the correct ascending sign with a birth time of an hour plus or minus factor on either side of the hours listed in these charts.

Chart six

Signs	Time	Pers.	Signs	Time	Pers.
2:00 To 4:00 AM			4:00 To 6:00 AM		
Aquar	↕	Sag	Aquar	↕	Cap
Pis	↕	Cap	Pis	↕	Aquar
Aries	↕	Aquar	Aries	↕	Pis
Tau	↕	Pis	Tau	↕	Aries
Gem	↕	Aries	Gem	↕	Tau
Can	↕	Tau	Can	↕	Gem
Leo	↕	Gem	Leo	↕	Can
Vir	↕	Can	Vir	↕	Leo
Lib	↕	Leo	Lib	↕	Vir
Sco	↕	Vir	Sco	↕	Lib
Sag	↕	Lib	Sag	↕	Sco
Cap	↕	Sco	Cap	↕	Sag

RELATIONSHIP CYCLES

All relationships have a beginning and an end. No matter what kind of relationship it is, marital, just friends, business, neighbors, they all have a starting point and they will all come to an end somewhere along the line in life. In this book we are dealing with personal involvements whether it is for love and sex, or just sex. These too, follow the same cycle as any other kind of joining. The cycle I am going to explain to you here may not take place exactly as I explain its events, but they will be close and you should heed them.

A relationship is a personal contract between you and another person no matter what kind of bonding it is. This kind of contract is represented by the seventh house in a person's chart, which, as you may recall is in opposition to the first house. The result of this opposition is that things that take place and form from the seventh house can work against you personally. The time the relationship starts is the birth of that relationship and this is when the life of relationship begins. It is also when the cycle begins. There are four stages for this cycle to flow through and I will explain them briefly for you.

Generally the first four years plus can go along smoothly, yet there may be some bumps along the way. Still things seem to be okay and continue. Near the four year and six month period, one of the parties may see, or meet someone they find of interest. Ideas of exploring a relationship with that person may, or may not take place, but a seed of interest has been planted. Astrologically this would be considered a squared aspect, or a period of potential trouble.

At nine years the relationship has reached an opposition to itself, or working against itself. At this time one, or both of the people involved, can again meet someone who stirs them in a meaningful manner. This could even be a renewed friendship from the past, or an entirely new one. This time, however, something could take place, something of an exploratory nature that can result in an ongoing liaison. This can of course bring the beginning of the end of the current involvement.

If the relationship has gotten through the nine-year part of the cycle, it will probably get through the next potential problem area which takes place at thirteen years six months, and you may wonder why they say thirteen is an unlucky number. This is again an astrological squared position to the beginning of the relationship and a time when a new person can enter the current relationship picture. Also it can be one that causes problems as it can stir the pot of feelings and sexual desires.

The critical portion of this cycle takes place at eighteen years and two months, plus or minus. This is known as the marriage cycle but it has the same affect on all relationships. The cycle itself has closed its loop from the starting point and so it has come to an end. More often than you might believe, this is when many personal and intimate lives will come to an end. The ending may be easy because both people understand what has happened, and that it is time to go in new directions. It can also end in bitterness. The kind of individual you have been involved with and had an understanding with may give you an indication of how it will end, and why.

If you have survived the 18.2 year cycle, odds are you will continue to survive in your relationship for years to come. Perhaps a lifetime.

HOUSE INFLUENCES
House Elements

There are twelve houses used in Astrology and in the delineation of natal charts. Each of them has some influence of a particular nature. Keep in mind that the leading edge of each house is known as the 'Cusp,' of that house, or the beginning of that house. Going in sequential order starting with the first house, they are as follows.

First house

This is the house of the physical being, and that of the body type. This is also where you find where the persons' personality originates, as well as their personal habits and outlook on life. The personality is most often formed by the age of seven though this may seem early to you, it is not. Often the illnesses' one suffers in life can be found associated with the sun sign found on this house cusp as well. Another thing to remember about this house is that we, as individuals, learn about love and intimacy from this location in our chart. This starts at birth and is most often understood by the child before the age of two years and four months. It is re-evaluated again between the years of twenty-eight, and thirty years four months. A time when some hard decisions are made as to the persons years ahead. At the age of fifty-six years to the age of fifty-eight years and four months, finds most people making yet another change in their life's direction. This could be the time you have to take a hard look at the retirement years ahead.

Second house

This is where the house where feelings about our personal possessions originates. Personal possessions will include anything in our lives, too include not only physical material items, but those of family as well. In a sense this is a house of personal inheritance that comes through the marriage, or possibly the loss thereof.

Surprising as it may seem to people, we learn about our own personal values between the ages of two years four months, and four years eight months. These values may face changes during a struggle period between the ages of thirty years four months, and thirty two years eight months. Again at the ages of fifty-eight years four months, to sixty years eight months. This is also a sexual house and the sun sign found on this house could be one of your more compatible sun sign considerations.

Third house

This is where the person learns their moral, philosophical, and religious beliefs, not to be confused with their theological views on life. This is found to be the house of communication, whether it is verbal or that of the written word. It also has an influence on short distance travel. We first learn how to communicate when we are between the ages of four years eight months and seven years. In a sense this concerns your neighborhood, especially as a child. This house also has to do with brothers and sisters. At the age of thirty-two years eight months to thirty-five years you are again going to experience this house, only this time you may move to a new area. This will bring new people into your life, and possibly new lovers as well.

Fourth house

This is where we learn about the honors, public opinions and reputations, as well as other ambitions of the person you are interested in getting to know better. These are things that come into play in lives between the ages of thirty-five and thirty-seven years four months. Though they are not restricted to this time frame as they could take place at a later time in life as well. The home life is found to be associated with this house. Also, the fathers influence, or that of a strong male influence, whether it is a father, grandfather, or that of an uncle. The fondness of the home is learned between the ages of seven years and nine years four months. It becomes a haven of safety from outside influences.

Fifth house

This is the house that has a strong tie to children, and ones love life. Love affairs can start here. The first one may have been between the ages of nine years four months to eleven years eight months. If you tell others about it at this young age, it will be passed off as an infatuation. If there is to be a love affair outside the marital union, it may start here. Also, to some degree, the taking of chances, or gambling of some kind. Our first loves might start here between the ages of nine years four months, to eleven years eight months.

Sixth house

If your love mate has a secret hidden away, or enemies, this is likely the hiding place. If they have issues with bad conduct, it can be found here as well. A stay in juvenile detention can come from this house as well. In a way you might look at this house as one of restrictions. More often than not, our first introduction to making an income of any kind, can start here between the ages of eleven years eight months, to fourteen years of age. It could be paper routes, or baby sitting. This house is known as the 'House of Servitude,' Which does not mean the person will be a servant in someone's household, it merely means a place where you learn what it is you might do in life to help others. It is also where some illnesses can be discovered. They will be the kind associated with the sun sign found on this house at the time of birth.

Seventh house

The seventh house represents partnerships of any kind, business, work related, or marital. It is also in opposition to the first house of self. This is, in a sense, a place of contracts. That is where agreements of some kind that you make, even though they may not be legally binding. So, in short, things that we do concerning the seventh house are not always good for ourselves. An example of this would be the ages of forty-two years to forty-four years four months. This is when most mid-life crisis's take place, why do they happen, you know why they do. Someone, or something else comes into our lives.

Eighth house

This is known as the house of death, though it may not be a physical death. It can just be where things come to an end. This is a sexual house and the sun sign found on this house could be one of your more compatible sun signs to consider. This could be old love affairs, past partnerships of any kind, and when you get here the third time in life at the ages of seventy years to seventy-two years four years four months, your sex life may well be over, or very near the end. This is the house of other people's money, which could be a won lottery, an inheritance, of something of the same sort. This is also the location of the partner's money or movable possessions.

Ninth house

The house of laws, moral and imagined. When you meet someone who is of devout theological beliefs, they will have planets in this house. The ninth house is also concerned with the marital family relations. This is the place people find themselves by age when they decide to get a higher education. Sometimes around the age of forty-six years to forty-nine years as this is when a lot of parents go back to school after their children are gone on to pursue their own lives, and now with the children gone they feel the need to finish learning a desired knowledge. This is the place where writers like to be found as it is the house of publications. This can be where their manner of speech is formed, the "Writer's Voice."

Tenth house

Professions are what this house is all about. Your choice of careers is often found here, though when you talk to people who are unhappy in their work, it may be a conflict of the sign on this house cusp and that of their first house cusp, self. All of your friends and relationships will now be those surrounded by this part of your life. Most often people are offered a vocational choice when they reach this house the first time at twenty years of age. The next time you pass through here you will find you are at the peak of your professional life, not necessarily the end of it, but the best part of it comes between the ages of forty-nine years and fifty-one years four months. If Venus is found in this house in someone's natal chart, odds are they will have love affairs with someone from their work office, or place of business.

Eleventh house

Friends are what the eleventh house is all about. Whether family, business, or professional. This too, is a sexual house and if you have Venus in this house it can cause problems. The problem is it may include anyone you know. Like the saying. "That's what friends are for." Why love one tree when you can love the whole forest?

Twelfth house

The place of secrets and hidden things, and most personal searches of any kind are found to originate here. It is the house of illusion, real, or imagined. If there are complications in the marital union the reasons may be found lurking here. If the persons' sun is found in this house at birth, they will be restricted in some manner by their mate. Physically or mentally. This is known as the place for hospital stays, even to go to jail or prison. This does not mean you will find yourself as a patient, or inmate, you could simply be one of the staff. If, however, you have not kept tract of your physical health, you cold find yourself under the scalpel and with a bright white light overhead.

MARRIAGE

Perhaps you've just met someone who has sparked your passionate, and intimate feelings. The chemistry of love, or lust takes control of your life and all reason goes right out the window. Perhaps you are not aware that there is a possibility that the chemistry can be wrong between the two of you.

The wanting of another person in our lives can lead us down the wrong path while seeking the correct mate. This often happens even when we already have a mate, or a commitment to someone currently in our lives. The problem encountered by most people is that they attempt to make themselves a couple with someone they have chosen, and perhaps even when their own personal needs do not match the other persons needs correctly.

With married couples, when one of the problem marriage cycles takes place it's often has the effect to end a seemingly sound marriage. Most of this takes place at a time when the couples are well established, financially, and domestically. A time that you, as an observer, would think all is well, and it may have been.

This particular cycle interrupts a marriage, often ending it, when it reaches the mature age of 18.2 years. There are many marriages that end before and after this time frame, but this particular cycle is consistent, and ongoing. There are several contributing factors, a few of which may pique your interest are discussed here.

In a sense, you would think the 18.2 year marital cycle would involve all marital age groups, but it does not. When you consider that one of the first age groups to suffer stressful times, regarding marriage, or seemingly solid relationships, is less than thirty years of age. An age factor that would require the couple to have started the relationship at the age of twelve. Still I once had a twelve-year-old Sagittarian tell me not to get married, but to wait for her. So, who knows?

The reasons for a divorce are usually caused by circumstances brought on by sexual infidelities, or incompatibilities due to mental growth. These are not the only reasons as money is a close runner up. The best possibility for a successful marriage the first time, is when the two people are over the age of twenty. At least the age of twenty for women and the age of twenty-three or four for men is best. Men much younger than this are, as a rule, just not ready for the marital commitment. Often it is simply because they are not mature enough. This is also why many women are drawn to older men.

DIVORCE

It is not unusual for two people to spend year after frustrated year with the wrong mate. Sometimes you will come across an older couple who just seem to live with each other, and they may just barely get along with one another. The constant bickering that takes place between them daily places their family in awkward positions. Even their children do not want to be around them because of the stress. Did they choose the wrong mate when they were younger, then stay together for the sake of the children? You know it happens, but what a shame and at a tremendous price. It could have been avoided by making a better choice in the beginning. It should also have come to an end long ago.

The more noticeable age cycle, for individuals to become divorced, is on average, 29.45 years. Friction in marriages for this age group starts when the individuals are about 26 years old. By the time they are age 28, they know many of the problems in their lives are being fueled, not only by themselves, but also by their marital, or sometimes non-marital mates. One, or the other involved in the marital partnership, will pull the plug on the relationship and seek a divorce, or at least seek an ending to the relationship. This particular age group often wants their freedom so badly, they seem to work against themselves in obtaining their freedom. When this happens, they place themselves in another seven-year cycle. This next seven-year cycle period involves personal struggles ranging from monetary, changing friendships, and perhaps even moving to a completely new area. After a parting of the ways has taken place, the two individuals now need to maintain two separate homes, and still be able to communicate with the ex-spouses family if children are involved.

TURNING THE CORNER

It may seem as though you will never be rid of the ongoing problems you encounter after a divorce, or the ending of a long term relationship. First it's as if you are completely alone in the world, then you find you can't make ends meet as your money just doesn't come in as fast as it goes out. There is however, a positive life cycle that starts about 35 years of age. This takes place after the six to seven year struggle period that came into your life about of the 29.45 year divorce cycle, and has been playing a heavy role in this part of your life. At this time the resistance from the past, and the struggles, will begin to fade away. This is turning the corner for many people, and a continuous upward spiral of better things to come. Well, almost. There is one more cycle to upset a few marriages, we know about this part of life, we call it the Mid-life crisis.

MID-LIFE CRISIS

In a sense you would think the 18.2 year marital cycle would be the end of this kind of stressful nonsense, but it isn't. It has been found that the next contributing demise to marriages is when one partner, or the other, enters what we've come to call, the mid-life crisis of life. Personal things start to take place at a point in a person's age, which seems as if it might be too late to make major changes in one's life style. You'll hear them say, "I've just got to find myself." Isn't it interesting to note that this generally falls about the age of 42-44? It isn't really, but it is part of the same cycle. However, it's as if we are working against ourselves, and against our own families. It seems as if it is a time for that fancy new sports car, and perhaps someone new has entered our lives, someone who catches our fancy and makes us feel younger than we really are.

In reality this is nearly what happens to each of us, yet it is slightly different for both the male, and female. In many cases, the ages may run from 42 to 46, more, or less. The male of our species is, at this age, is trying to maintain his virility and his ability to attract women, especially women younger than himself. It seems that this is the last chance at being a competing male. At the same time, he wants to keep what he has worked all his life to attain. Still he takes the chance, possibly throwing it all away for one last fling at life. Often a very costly fling.

170

The female however, is just now reaching a point in her life where she is experiencing her greatest sexual fulfillment. This is a time when she has cast away the inhibitions from earlier years. Now she finds out she can really enjoy a sexual partner. She puts her all into the relationship, and may even devour a man who has thought of her as timid, or withdrawn.

THE LAST CHANCE

For those of us, who may have not made the change for the better at the age of 29 years, when we reach the age of 56 it seems to be the last chance to rid ourselves of a bad relationship. Or, we have one last chance to start anew.

LOOKING AGAIN

A contributing factor to many of these problems is another cycle we hear little about. This is a curse of mankind in general; male or female it does not matter. It is a cycle that interferes with our lives, though it may be one of the unconscious mind. Its influence is one that brings many unhappy situations to bear. It does not seem to matter that you may have a mate already, its nature's way. If you are single, this cycle may not have a profound impact on your life, as this cycle is one that takes place every seven or eight years. That is, the looking for a new mate.

YOUR MARITAL BLISS, OR IS IT?
Why is it some marriages are alive, and very healthy while others die miserably? Often the reasons are quite simple; it is a matter of understanding where you are in your life. To some folks this may seem a foreign thought, but the outcome of your marriage may depend on where you and your mate are in your individual life cycles. You, as the reader, need to read through this book to decide who you really are, and what Sun sign might be best for you. Self honesty is crucial, and though some of the Sun signs you may read about sound like an exciting possibility to you, take care, it might be a good time at your expense. None of the Sun signs are perfect, though many of them will think they are.

There are a few lucky people who seem to find a life's soul mate for life. We see them in supermarkets, on the sidewalks, in the parks, they are the couple holding hands as they walk along. It's not a put on, and it's real. It is easy to see they are walking life's path together. Where you find one, you find the other, it's as if they never want to be apart. Most just seem to have been lucky, but it's really the wise person who has chosen their mate carefully.

SECTION THREE

This section may be more easily understood if you have a natal chart on the individual you are researching. Still, the information will be of value to you with just having it handy and being able to refer back to it from time to time.

THE TROUBLE IS. . .

Not only is Venus a problem in some signs, it may also be more of a problem in any one of the twelve houses. Venus indicates where the love, or enjoyments of life, come into play. Remember that enjoyments often lead to an over indulgence in whatever gives us pleasure. The house position can tell you how those influences may take place. Let's discuss the heavier natal house impacts of Venus first, and then we will review the remaining houses. As you read this, you will find the houses are not listed in sequential order.

VENUS IN THE FIRST HOUSE OF PERSONALITY

With Venus in the first house, the high sexual drive becomes more apparent. It is more difficult having Venus in this house because it is now a personal and a physical influence. Venus in any house will cause over indulgence in those related parts of life, but here in has to do with the individual's physical being, and drive.

Most of the problems encountered will involve the attitude, and the opinions of the person, and either of these can cause problems.

The attitude is that they want to fulfill their desires and cravings regardless of the personal costs to their private, or public life. Their opinion is that they can fulfill these cravings no matter the problems it may cause them, or those close to them.

The direction in which Venus searches for gratification can depend on whether it is the chart of a male, or female, and the influence of the constellation it is in. The placement of the sun or moon in the natal chart will show the other directions of how Venus will spread her tentacles to engulf the rest of the charts potential. In a woman's chart, whatever house the sun resides in, is where her Venus will look for sexual gratification. In the male's chart, it will be wherever the moon resides.

174

If the sexual cravings, and desires are held in check, the effects of Venus can take place in other ways. Such as overeating, often a tool used to make oneself less appealing to the opposite sex, but furthers the actual need. Or, starving ones self to look better. Perhaps the use of alcohol, or drugs if a water sign inhabits the first house cusp. Most often the individual will seek a solution that affects the physical body in some manner, and it will be done with pleasure in mind.

The cravings brought about because of a first house Venus, will be apparent when a person wakes up in the morning and only end when they go to sleep at night. When the addiction is to food or drink, it is all they think about, if it is sex, the same condition is true.

The restlessness can be overwhelming. This first house of the physical body can cause addiction to anything that will bring pleasure to the individual. It matters not what the addiction is composed of, or whether it is good or bad for a person. Even age has little effect, just because the body starts to slow down, as with an older person, the mind does not.

It does happen, a person has Venus in the first house, and they struggle, but learn to mute the condition. However, the addition will often show up in some other form.

VENUS IN ARIES IN THE FIRST HOUSE
This may very well be the most assertive lover.
One who will pursue their intended playmate with
vigilance. This will not be a shy individual, if you
are their intended desire, you will be made aware
of their interest in you. Yet, they will not waste
much time on a pursuit that seems to be lacking in
mutual interest. This, is a busy lover, one who
jumps into a relationship quickly, and may look for
another lover just as quickly.

VENUS IN SCORPIO IN THE FIRST HOUSE
Undoubtedly, you've heard of the Nymphomaniac,
Well the first house of physical body, is where that
person's Venus is likely to be found. Venus in
Scorpio is bad enough, but in the first house, it
may be insatiable. Should you choose to spend
time with this person, be aware most of it may be
spent in bed, or something that serves the same
purpose. If you choose this lover, and were wrong
in doing so, you will find yourself way out of your
league. This is a strong and intense lover.

VENUS IN CAPRICORN IN THE FIRST HOUSE
As this is a very social sun sign, but love affairs
with this person will have to be very discreet. This
is someone who not only wants their cake, and a
second helping, perhaps even a third. That is,
relationships outside of their normal domestic

commitments can, and often will, happen. There may be more than one going at the same time. When they are ready to make love nothing else matters.

VENUS IN AQUARIUS IN THE FIRST HOUSE
Venus in Aquarius is the last of these four heavier sexual signs of the Zodiac. Aries, Scorpio, Capricorn, and Aquarius. With Aquarius being a free thinker, and someone who thinks everyone deserves equal treatment like they themselves give others. And, yes, they give themselves to lovers. But not to just anyone person, it could be everyone they take a fancy too.

VENUS IN THE THIRD HOUSE
This house location of Venus can show a love of travel, and communicating, such as writing novels or short stories. It will also involve a variety of individuals in this person's love life. The love experiences could come from their travels abroad, or at home. This is the house ruled by Gemini, hence duality. In this case, the duality may take its pleasure from several sources.

The third house love life can be very close to home, and very personal, which is where brothers and sisters come into play. Yes, that includes adopted brothers and sisters, even cousins. The third house rules relatives, and with Venus in the third house it can also bring about unwanted attention from a step parent. Outside of the personal home life, the Venus effect may include love affairs with an Acquaintance, such as a neighbor.

Those with Venus in the third house are also very good at talking about sex, and it can be with anyone. Person to person, over the telephone, over the internet, or whatever. These are the people who can stir sexual emotions readily with the spoken word, and they do so with offending the opposite sex.

VENUS IN THE TWELFTH HOUSE
The twelfth house Venus location concerns hidden things, things that are kept hidden by the people involved, such as cheating on one's mate, but it can go much deeper than that.

The problem most often encountered is that for some reason, we as individuals, cannot keep our mouths shut. If we have a secret love affairs we will tell someone else about it, then our unknown love life will soon be known by someone else, and of course it doesn't stop there. Pride in our ability to attract the opposite sex, can be costly.

With secret love affairs, the people involved are faced with a constant stream of lies, and the fear of getting caught, and of course being found out is usually the end result. In a sense, those involved often inform on themselves. Love affairs bring trouble for this Venus position, sometimes danger is also close at hand.

It requires an unusual understanding between the two lovers to avoid a serious social downfall. A secure knowledge between them that this thing they have going is strictly an affair, and nothing else. That there is no long term plan to divorce their current mates, and ultimately to wed one another. Though this, does happen.

The successful Venus in the twelfth house love affair takes place with the understanding that they both know this is for the fun of enjoying a different lover for the time. In the end, the secret love affair caused by Venus being placed in the twelfth house will come to an end. If it is a controlled love affair, as mentioned above, it will end without total unhappiness, and the destruction of two entire families.

One last thing to consider as a curse of Venus in this house, is that prostitution can take over the love life, and direct the individual in a whole new lifestyle. This of course brings many unhappy situations to bear, and the diseases that can get passed along may only be the tip of the iceberg. Those who enjoy bondage and masochism, often have Venus in this house, or a suffering in some manner, something that is not brought out into the public eye. This life style, when one gets caught up in it, can truly be a curse.

VENUS IN THE FIFTH HOUSE

This is the house that rules love, it is also the house of children, your own, or those you adopt. Also it is the house of romances, with your spouse or with someone else's. You guessed it, this can be the house of promiscuity. A personal problem that can last a lifetime. A person with Venus here can fight the tendency, but, depending on the sign Venus is in at birth, it may be a losing battle.

This house position of Venus brings with it a great deal of ongoing social events. There is a tendency to gamble, or to take chances of some kind. Lovers can easily come from this house, as well as any kind of sensuous enjoyments. Sexuality is fully enjoyed by this person and it can involve sexual relationships in, or out of the home.

VENUS IN THE SECOND HOUSE

Venus indicates an enjoyment for whatever house, or sign it is in. As the second house is monetary, the enjoyment will be for financial well being. This can be a personal drive that can upset other family members. It will do so because of the drive to obtain whatever it is they want matters so much to the individual that it can consume them.

Probably the most important thing to this kind of person, is the monetary freedom they know exists. No matter how it comes about, this person wants it for their own. This, is a person who may marry just to enjoy the wealth of the marital partner, The importance here is in material possessions. Be it homes, cars, or anything else of value. Will this person enjoy it, you can bet they will try? Will someone with this Venus position be rich, perhaps, but, probably not.

Odds are that once they get the financial means to do, as they want, they will not give it away to anyone else on purpose. This financial freedom may come about through their personal endeavors, or it could just as easily come from the death of a partner, business or marital. You might think of someone with this kind of outlook as a cold and calculating person, but this is not necessarily the case. As the second house is often thought of as a sexually stimulated house as well.

VENUS IN THE FOURTH HOUSE

A fourth house Venus is one of interest as it covers some unusual items, but mostly it is about the home, and the home life. It is concerned with the individuals personal home, or that of family estates. With Venus here, the living conditions will reflect the pleasures that the owner enjoys most. Among other things, there will be an area, somewhere in the home, that keeps any of the personal secrets, or belongings of its occupants, keeps them safely hidden away. Venus in this house can indicate losses caused by losses from a love affair that has ended badly. These love affairs, may have been an unstable affair in the beginning, as this Venus position encounters strange events in love and marriage.

This person's intimate thoughts and concerns, may reflect the fact that they feel any older person in their family, should be allowed to live in the home with the younger family. This could be anyone from and an aunt or an uncle, to one's parents and at least, older family members. The living conditions for the elderly person will be greatly improved by this relationship.

VENUS IN THE SIXTH HOUSE

Venus in the sixth house can bring a discovery, and the enjoyment of doing things for others. Often to the point of self denial. Is the self-denial something the individual consciously desires, of course not, but this person is someone who thinks about the needs of others. This, is a person who thinks that others need help before they actually get around to doing things for themselves. You may see indications of them thinking this way and not recognize it right away. Such as a grandparent who living on a fixed income. Most of the time they can barely pay their own housing costs, and their medications put a tremendous strain on their bank account, if they have one. Yet, if there is a grandchild in need of a pair of shoes, the child will have them. Never mind how many meals the cost of the shoes may have provided for the grandparents.

If it isn't their grandchildren they are spending their money on, it could just as easily be animals, large or small. The animals will be spoiled, just as if they were grandchildren. New horseshoes for the horses, shots for the cats or dogs. A cat or dog will have a very plush bed to sleep in, even if they seldom use it for that purpose. Whatever emotional project it is, that sucks the lifeblood away from this person, it will enjoy the comforts of love.

More so in youth than in later years, with Venus in this house sexually transmitted diseases may have to be considered, and dealt with at some point in life. Of course, it can be expensive to suffer this malady, perhaps as high as costing a marriage.

VENUS IN THE SEVENTH HOUSE

Venus makes friends' wherever it resides at the time of your birth. When Venus is found in the seventh house, it brings out alliances that result in odd circumstances. The relationships can be between women friends, and men friends, or perhaps it is just conjugal affection between two people, rather than a passionate love affair between sweethearts.

Something to think about is the fact that when Venus is in the seventh house it is also in opposition to the first house, which represents the person to whom the chart belongs. What this amounts to, is that the person may work against themselves by becoming involved in love affairs that may not be good for them. If you are involved in one of these kinds of relationships, take care in how you part company, as Venus in this house can result in personal enemies in the long run.

Secret relationships between two lovers will often result in divorce between them and their marital mates. More often than not, this will be done to change life's partners, rather than divorcing to satisfy the anger of the current mate.

This kind of relationship can result in a divorce that catches the marital partner completely off guard. The surprise comes because the marital partner may have felt all was well in his or her personal relationship.

The new relationship may start with a simple chance meeting involving a perfect stranger, yet a meeting that blossoms and grows much farther, and faster, than expected.

VENUS IN THE EIGHTH HOUSE

The problems caused by Venus in this house will depend largely upon which sign Venus is in. As this is the house that rules the sexual organs, it is a strong sexual house to begin with. Then you add a heavy Venus, such as Venus in Aries, Scorpio, or Capricorn, and you have a power to be reckoned with.

The eighth house also rules the end of things and can contribute to the ending of relationships, marital or business. Someone with Venus in the eighth house may end up paying alimony for years because of the infidelities starting from a sexual affair. There is a side to Venus being in this house that is often overlooked. Ones love life can come to an end here as well. It may simply be an age factor. Or a harsher side may result in someone's being in a relationship where the partner simply stops participating in the sexual act. It can also indicate someone who finds it difficult to enjoy sex.

The kind of relationships that can form from this Venus position will often be with friends from the past part of your life. Perhaps someone you were intimate with as a younger person suddenly shows up, and you get together for lunch, or dinner. The first thing you know it's having breakfast together, well you see where this is going.

VENUS IN THE NINTH HOUSE

This is not a house of high sexual needs, but with Venus residing here in the natal chart, it can be a curse non-the-less. Venus in this house may bring a love to travel, and not just around the neighborhood. Countries, and continents yes. This exploring may be disguised as something leading to a higher education, or it may be that the person just likes to travel.

This condition can bring with it some strange, or secret love affairs. The problem arises when the Venus travel effect, affects the family life, as this person is never home to take care of their home love life. This being the case, while they are gone, their loved ones may be doing a bit of exploring on their own. Searching for someone, who will be around in the evenings and weekends. It doesn't have to be a traveler who is never home, it could just as easily be someone studying on a continual basis.

As an example, it could be someone who is just beginning a career in the legal circles. Lawyers are notorious for spending endless hours at the office, all in the name of profession, and career. It doesn't have to be a student of Law, but it can be any form of higher learning. A science of some kind, perhaps even that of a teacher who spends hours correcting tests, or getting the next class material ready for the upcoming class and the students.

VENUS IN THE TENTH HOUSE

The tenth house Venus is, or can be, another form of promiscuity. The career, or profession takes place first, then the family may come next. The ambition for advancement is expensive in the terms of ones love life. There is every indication there will be an office affair, these too, can be expensive in some manner. You have to pay the price eventually; it is only a matter of which it is you want to keep the family, or the career. If the rewards in the profession can result in fame, the family may have to wait, as the spotlight is hard to turn your back on.

Life can be tough on this kind of individual, because they think their mates do not understand them. It is this person, who has to make up their mind as to their goals in life, and its costs to them personally.

VENUS IN THE ELEVENTH HOUSE

Venus here is seldom a problem, unless one's mate is suffering from emotional neglect, as the lack of a loving companion does take a toll. It could be that this is a person who gives all of their love to children. Perhaps personal acquaintances, or other friendly companions, rather than giving it to their own mate. This may also be the mate who creates love problems into the marriage. Perhaps it's simply because they lack the knowledge to figure out what their own mate needs in the way of love, and, or affections. It is not unusual for someone with Venus in the eleventh house to marry into a ready-made family.

TROUBLE FROM PLANETS IN THE SEVENTH HOUSE

The planets we discuss in this part do not necessarily cause problems themselves alone, but when coupled with conditions from other planets, they can create trouble in someone's life. It is conditions caused by other planets in the chart to planets in the seventh house that are of importance. One of the problems of planets in the seventh house is that you may not see the harsh effects of the planet until after you marry, or form a partnership of some kind with these people. If you should end up with a partner who has one of these conditions in their chart, it can seem a cursed situation.

Sometimes the biggest problems arise from planets located in the first or twelfth houses. The first house because it affects the personal side of the individual as well as the physical. The twelfth house because it brings out hidden things. These hidden things can produce dramatic influences in any relationship.

SUN

The Sun in the seventh house can produce a partner who may be domineering. Perhaps even selfish, or too extravagant in their life style. If you marry someone who has the Sun in the seventh house as a step toward a higher social standing, it can be a very expensive step. A person who has the Sun in the seventh house may not marry until later in life, this happens often because of the fires that burn within. A feeling can reside in this person that prevents them from settling down to a fixed lifestyle.

MOON

The relationships the Moon and the other planets in the chart are of importance. If you choose someone with the Moon in the seventh house, you may find yourself with a moody partner. This can also be a partner, who will possibly stray from the marital bed. The Moon in this house of one's horoscope does not indicate a successful marriage the first time. The second marriage will have a better chance at survival.

This is a good Moon position for a parent with children in the home, but it can make the partnership a real problem. This may also bring a mate who is greedy and ready to take anything within reach. As the ruler of the Sun sign Cancer, the Moon can bring a partner into your life, who nags you a great deal of the time. Perhaps one who insists that you agree with his or her line of thinking. Often, a partner in this kind of relationship will give in, just to keep the peace.

MERCURY

Remember, this is the planet of communication we are discussing here, and with this planet in the seventh house, it can produce a partner who is talkative and flirtatious. Yet, their mind will remain true to the marriage, and to the marital partner. Mercury in this house can produce a mate who is younger, perhaps even a distant relative, or a past school friend. Either of these conditions will bring their relatives influence into the family as well.

If you yourself have Mercury in this house and if the planetary relationship to Mercury is harsh, you may tend to attract a partner who is constantly talking, or nagging.

 Make your decision before the union takes place, as Mercury in this position can produce a relationship where steady bickering, or quarreling is commonplace. If those same conditions exist and cause problems, and should a divorce start to take place, you, as the marital partner, may want to guard your bank account. It could disappear quickly if left unguarded.

VENUS

If Venus has good relationships with the other planets while in this house, it will be a very good indication of a warm and loving relationship. If not, it can bring a disappointing mate into your life. Among other things this may not be a neat and tidy type person. If, Venus is in one of the fire signs, Aries, Leo, or Sagittarius, it may bring with it a partner who has a detached view toward the marriage. In the case of Leo, it can be the best of the fire signs for Venus to be in, in the seventh house. Venus in Aries can be a mate who requires a mate to keep up with, or meet their sexual needs. Venuses in Pisces, Cancer, or Taurus, in the seventh house, may be the best astrological signs for compatibility in the marriage.

MARS

The planet Mars in the seventh house can bring about spontaneous, and irregular love affairs. Mars in this house can also cause arguments, perhaps even accidents, or disruptions of any kind. In short, this is not a good planet to have in the seventh house.

Mars here can attract a partner to you who may seem ideal, but more often Mars brings with it a danger to the person who has Mars in their seventh house.

If Mars is in a water sign in your personal seventh house, you may be someone who is constantly drawn to partners who drink excessively. If this is the case in your natal chart, you may be the one who has been heard to say, "Why do I always choose this kind." Well Mars in a water sign is the reason, and it will seem like an ongoing problem and self realization needs to take place.

JUPITER

As a general rule with Jupiter in the seventh house, marital or natal it does bring some ability to protect the individual, and the marriage. However, if Jupiter is not well situated with respects to the other planets, it can bring about not only bad luck, but in some cases, tremendous misfortune. Jupiter will often allow the individual to choose the wrong mate for their life. It can also indicate someone who will have numerous affairs of the heart, before, during, and after marriage.

SATURN

This can be a problem planet for any seventh house partnership. Saturn in this house, can, and often does, cause the loss of a mate, perhaps even denying marriage for some years. A normal reaction in life is that when Saturn is found in the natal chart's seventh house, it brings about a marriage between two people who have a large difference in ages between them. Ten years is quite common, and twenty years' differences can happen as well. Often this is only a problem if the age difference causes some end of life problems for the mate left to fend for him, or herself.

It can just as easily bring a marital union in which one of the partners is of a cold nature. If this is the case, the one with the natal Saturn in the seventh house, should consider getting a divorce. Good luck if this is the case, because; this may be a marital partner who refuses, for one reason or the other, to agree to a divorce.

URANUS

One of the dangers of having Uranus in the seventh house is the odd, or unusual circumstance surrounding the possible mate chosen. Uranus in this house does not really favor marriage, as it instills a certain need for freedom from restrictions of any kind. Though the partner chosen is often above average in intelligence, and may understand the other's needs. This planet is more favorable to marriage when placed in a woman's seventh house rather than a man's, because in a man's chart it can bring a possibility of homosexuality. If Uranus is not harmonious with the other planets, you can expect the marriage to fall apart, and why would anyone stay together when neither of them can be happy?

NEPTUNE

Is this person happy in their marriage? It may seem so to others, but we are dealing with Neptune here. Odds are, there will be some dissatisfaction in the marriage, whether the conditions causing the problems are real, or imagined. This is the planet of deception, and it can produce a marital partner that may seem unknown, even to the mate. The real person with this Neptune position may never be truly known to their mates, or anyone else. It is not unusual for this marital partner to desert the marriage without explanation, or prior notice. The old saying of 'Here today, gone tomorrow,' can easily fit this Neptune placement.

The person with Neptune in the seventh house, is often someone who self sacrifices themselves for the mate, at least that can be the way they see the situation. Their mate may be someone who is pitied, perhaps needs to be nursed through the years, even locked away somewhere. When the wrong kind of marriage is entered into, it can be a total waste. Normally this marriage will end, and rightly so.

PLUTO

Pluto usually shows a need, so when you find someone with Pluto in the seventh house, it indicates a person needs a mate in their life. With Pluto in this house, it can bring someone into the relationship that seems sensuous in their very nature. Pluto in this house can change a mate from a stick in the mud, to an erotic lover. Pluto is a planet which brings changes, and generally for the better.

LOVERS OF THE SIXTH and TWELFTH HOUSE
The Astrological signs that fall on the sixth and twelfth house cusps of a chart, are good, or bad, depending on how, or when they begin to effect a persons life. Both the sixth and twelfth houses are restrictive houses; thus both Sun signs that fall on these house cusps can be restrictive signs to the native. Generally, relationships with people of these signs are trouble from the beginning, though at the time one may not think of them as such. But once you cross some line, and only they know where it is, all hell can break loose. As a rule these are two Sun signs a person should not get involved with for long term relationships. Short term, associations may work out, but don't bet on it.

Look at your own personal chart, and remember that communications between yourself and the people who are of the Sun signs found on your sixth and twelfth houses, may be misunderstood. Perhaps even wantonly disregarded, either of which can cause complicated problems later. Most of the time an intimate relationship with one of the Sun signs found on the twelfth house will not normally be known about, as they will be hidden relationships from the beginning. The problems that can be caused are not openly known by many of those acquainted with the two people involved. But complications can arise that will be demanding in some manner.

The sign on the sixth house can cause problems as well, but these relationships will come before the public's eye in some manner. You would think any problems caused by the sign on the twelfth house would be seen by the public as well but this is not the case. However, the sign on the sixth house seems to demand some public attention.

ASPECTS

When pursuing someone of your choosing, aspects will be something to consider. As an example, when any planet is in the first house, it is in its most powerful position if it is within the first ten degrees of the first house cusp. When it is Venus you must consider the sign it is in and the intensity of that sign. If it is not a highly sexual sign for Venus and you attempt to make yourself desirable to this person, you may be wasting your time if you choose the wrong time to approach them.

The moon is most often the triggering planet that sets things in motion. The information I'm telling you about here is when the moon is making the aspects to Venus, or any planet for that matter. The aspects of semi-sextile, sextile, semi-square, square, and the in-conjunction, do not always appear to work well and to your advantage. The opposition may prove fruitful, but don't count on it. The most effectual aspect to use is when the moon is in a trine aspect to Venus in the first house.

The better trine is found to be the one from the fifth house of love. When using the moon's aspect to a planet you must remember the moon travels fast so you cannot waste time to make up your mind about the pursuit. Either you are going ahead with your choice, or you are not.

IFPublications
mgn.editor@gmail.com

Other books written by Donald Boone

Two free natal charts are available if you are the original purchaser of the book, Sexual Happiness or Choosing Lovers.. Contact for details can be made through the e-mail address listed above.

SEXUAL HAPPINESS

Sexual happiness is one of the most important things to happen in your life. This book is designed to help you look for the correct person to have in your life. This kind of search is seldom preformed, but it should be the case in every relationship. Be honest with yourself about your own needs, then use this book to find the best lover to fill your own life.

ISBN 1-882896-16-5
EAN 978-1882896-16-5

CHOOSING LOVERS
Why spend years with the wrong lover. Find the one that best suits your needs and enjoy freedom from sexual hunger.
ISBN 1-882896-04-1
EAN 978-1-882896-04-2

CYCLES & RHYTHMS of INTRIGUE
Most of life, if not all of it, contains cycles.
From the birth of any event it will find
its natural rhythm and follow it to the
end. Is life fated, read the answer in this
book.
ISBN 1-882896-07-6
EAN 978-1-882896-07-3

THE CHESS COACH
Becoming one is easy, and it can be
very rewarding. If you play the game
and have time on your hands, consider
becoming a chess coach.
ISBN 1-882896-08-4
EAN 978-1882896-08-0

THE SEA PILOT
In this age of sailing vessels, we no longer fear sailing
over the edge of the flat world, and we find our way
with compass and chronometer. This was not so when
this story took place.
ISBN 1-882896-09-2
EAN 978-1-882896-09-7

CHESS STORIES THROUGH THE AGES
This book, 'Chess Stories Through The Ages,'
contains stories that have been passed from one
generation to the next down through history. From why
'White moves first, and an unknown story of 'Helen of
Troy, found in, 'The Sacrificed Trojan Horse.'
ISBN 1-882896-10-6
EAN 978-1882896-10-3

THOSE WHO PLAY CHESS

Knowing how your opponent plays chess, his or her favorite pieces and their quirks, are a definite advantage to you in this game. Especially if you play in tournaments. This book will provide you with information on them as individuals, and that of their personalities. You will also find lists of historical players with the same kinds of individualism's and personalities to help guide you in your defense at the table.

ISBN 1-882896-11-4
EAN 978 -1-882896 -11-0

IMPACT

Meteors have been haunting mankind since the beginning of mankind, and they still do. This story is about one of those celestial bodies that does not miss the earth on its path around our sun. Like meteorites of the past, the damage it causes when it strikes the earths surface, is devastating. However, many survive and this story is about how one group came together to get through the worst of the affects.

ISBN 1-882896-12-2
EAN 978-1-882896-12-7

THE CHESS GAME

Having lost a huge sum in prize money due to an oversight in a championship chess game, he became a revenge killer. He spelled it out for his opponents during his killing spree. You will see the connection as you read this story.

ISBN 1-882896-13-0
EAN 978-1882896-13-4

WELCOME ABOARD

When those who have lived around the water, and their day comes to an end, it is time to relax. Whether they are lying in a Vee birth, or on a cushion in the cockpit of a boat. Perhaps even a bed ashore. It doesn't matter as they frequently have an abundance of time. To fill the time they read and let the stories unfold in their mind's as the hours pass by. This book is comprised of stories that take place in this world. A place where you meet life on its terms.

ISBN 1-882896-03-3
EAN 978-1-882896-03-5